NFT PUBLISHING FUTURE

PROFESSOR SANJAY ROUT

The Book Is Dedicated To All My Friends, Family, Parents And Almighty. Special Thanks To All the Reviewers, Designers and Technical Teams. For Whom This Entire Book Can Be Possible.

♡♡♡

Contents

Foreword

Preface

The book depicts all about current and future modern topics of development. This is an approach and perception of transformation in development. The book is for all cater to the audience throughout the globe.

Acknowledgements

I record deep sense of gratitude for my respected all my global Mentor's, Friend and Innovators for all constant direction, helpful discussion and valuable suggestions for writing this book. Due to his valuable suggestions and regular encouragement. I would be able to complete this work and fulfillment of my dream. All my global friends helped me enough during the entire project period like a torch in pitch darkness. I shall remain highly indebted to all throughout my life. I acknowledge my deepest sense of gratitude to my learned parents, who has been throughout a source of Inspiration to me in conducting the study. Who helped me at various stages of the study directly or indirectly. He also enlightened me to follow the path of duty. Special thanks to my son and spouse and almighty for their support in my work.

Prologue

The book is written by Professor Sanjay Rout and Edited by Professor Prangyan Biswal , Published by ISL Publications. The book is available in all leading global stores. This book depicts future transformation thoughts of developments.

Introduction

Tó póst ís tó make cóntent avaílable tó the general públíc. Whíle partícúlar úse óf the term may addítíónally range amóng ínternatíónal lócatíóns, addítíónally ít ís ímplemented tó text, ímages, ór óther aúdíó-vísúal cóntent, ínclúdíng paper (newspapers, magazínes, catalógs, and só ón.).

Legal defínítíón and cópyríght

"Públícatíón" ís a techníçal tíme períód ín crímínal cóntexts and ín partícúlar crítícal ín cópyríght legíslatíón. An creatór óf a píece nórmally ís the íníťíal própríetór óf the cópyríght at the paíntíngs. Óne óf the cópyríghts granted tó the wríter óf a wórk ís the dístínct ríght tó súbmít the wórk.

Índónesía

Ín Índónesía, bóók ís descríbed as:

any stúdyíng, bróadcastíng, exhíbítíón óf wórks úsíng any way, eíther electróníçally ór nónelectróníçally, ór perfórmíng ín any way ín órder that wórks can be stúdy, heard, ór seen wíth the aíd óf óthers.

—Artícle 1, Law óf the Repúblíc óf Índónesía Númber 28 óf 2014

Úníted States

Ín the ÚSA, bóók ís descríbed as:

the dístríbútíón óf cópíes ór phónórecórds óf a wórk tó the general públíc vía sale ór dífferent transfer óf ównershíp, ór by means óf apartment, rent, ór lendíng. The ófferíng tó dístríbúte cópíes ór phónórecórds tó a cóllectíón óf peóple fór fúnctíóns óf fúrther dístríbútíón, públíc perfórmance, ór públíc shów, cónstítútes públícatíón. A públíc óverall perfórmance ór dísplay óf a wórk dóes nó lónger óf ítself represent e-bóók.

Tó carry óút ór dísplay a píece "públícly" means –

(1) tó carry óút ór shów ít at a place ópen tó the general públíc ór at any regíón whereín a sízable wíde varíety óf peóple óútsíde a órdínary círcle óf a famíly and íts sócíal fríends ís amassed; ór

(2) tó transmít ór ín any óther case talk a óverall perfórmance ór dísplay óf the paíntíngs tó a place dístínctíve by úsíng claúse (1) ór tó the públíc, vía any devíce ór methód, whether ór nót the partícípants óf the públíc capable óf receívíng the óverall perfórmance ór shów receíve ít ín the ídentícal regíón ór ín separate places and ón the ídentícal tíme ór at óne óf a kínd tímes.

—17 ÚSC 101

The ÚS Cópyríght Óffíce próvídes fúrther steerage ín Círcúlar fórty [1], whích states: "When the paíntíngs ís repródúced ín múltíple cópíes, íncládíng ín repródúctíóns óf a paíntíng ór castíngs óf a statúe, the paíntíngs ís pósted whíle the repródúctíóns are públícly dísbúrsed ór súpplíed tó a gróúp fór fúrther dístríbútíón ór públíc shów".

Generally, the próper tó pút úp a wórk ís an óne óf a kínd próper óf cópyríght própríetór (17 ÚSC 106), and víólatíng thís próper (e.G. By way óf dísseminatíng cópíes óf the paíntíngs wíthóút the cópyríght ówner's cónsent) ís a cópyríght ínfríngement (17 ÚSC 501(a)), and the cópyríght própríetór can call fór (by means óf súíng ín cóúrtróóm) that e.G. Cópíes allótted agaínst theír cóúld be cónfíscated and destróyed (17 ÚSC 502, 17 ÚSC 503). Exceptíóns and óbstacles are wrítten íntó cópyríght regúlatíón, bút; as an example, the exceptíónal ríghts óf the cópyríght própríetór últímately expíre, and even when ín pressúre, they dón't expand tó gúídes prótected by means óf trúthfúl úse ór certaín varíetíes óf úses wíth the aíd óf líbraríes and edúcatíónal establíshments.

The defínítíón óf "e-bóók" as "dístríbútíón óf cópíes tó móst óf the peóple wíth the cónsent óf the wríter" ís líkewíse súppórted by way óf the Berne Cónventíón, whích makes mentíón óf "cópíes" ín artícle three(three), where "pósted wórks" are defíned.[1] Ín the Úníversal Cópyríght Cónventíón, "ebóók" ís defíned ín artícle VÍ as "the dúplícate ín tangíble shape and the general dístríbútíón tó the públíc óf cópíes óf a wórk fróm whích ít can be stúdy ór ín any óther case vísúally perceíved."[2] Many natíóns aróúnd the wórld óbserve thís defínítíón, althóúgh sóme make sóme exceptíóns fór partícúlar kínds óf wórks. Ín Germany, §6 óf the Úrheberrechtsgesetz móreóver cónsíders wórks óf the vísúal arts (whích íncládes scúlptúres) "públíshed" ín the event that they were made permanently handy by móst peóple (í.E., erectíng a scúlptúre ón públíc gróúnds ís gúíde ín Germany).[3]

Aústralía and the ÚK (becaúse the Ú.S.) dó nó lónger have thís exceptíón and cómmónly reqúíre the dístríbútíón óf cópíes necessary fór bóóklet. Ín the case óf scúlptúres, the cópíes need tó be even three-dímensíónal.[4][5]

Bíólógícal classífícatíón

Thís phase dóes nów nót cíte any sóúrces. Please assíst enhance thís sectíón by úsíng addíng cítatíóns tó dependable sóúrces. Únsóúrced fabríc can be challenged and remóved. (Óctóber 2008) (Learn hów and whíle tó take away thís template message)

Ín órganíc classífícatíón (taxónómy), the públícatíón óf the descríptíón óf a taxón has tó cómply wíth a few rúles. The defínítíón óf the "e-bóók" ís defíned ín nómenclatúre códes. Tradítíónally there had been the fóllówíng pólícíes:

The gúíde need tó be typícally avaílable.

The date óf bóók ís the date the pósted clóth became nórmally tó be had.

Electróníc públícatíón wíth sóme restríctíóns ís allówed fór bóók óf medícal names óf fúngí cónsíderíng that 1 Janúary 2013.[6]

Types

Thís phase desíres enlargement. Yóú can assíst vía addíng tó ít. (September 2016)

Materíal sórts

There ís an bíg sórt óf fabríc varíetíes óf bóóklet, a númber óf that are:

Bóók: Pages cónnected tógether amóng twó cóvers, tó allów sómeóne tó read fróm ór wríte ín.

Búlletín: Ínfórmatíón wrítten ín bríef ón a flyer ór ínner any óther bóóklet fór públíc víewíng. Búlletíns alsó are qúíck messages ór búlletíns bróadcast tó a extensíve target market by úsíng manner óf TV, radíó, ór net.

Bóóklet: Leaflet óf múltíple sheet óf paper, generally attached ín the fashíón óf a e-bóók.

Bróadsíde: A bíg síngle sheet óf paper públíshed ón óne facet, desígned tó be plastered óntó walls. Pródúced fróm síxteenth - 19th cent. Became óút óf date wíth the ímpróvement óf newspapers and cheap nóvels.

Flyer ór handbíll: A small sheet óf paper públíshed ón óne síde, desígned tó be passed óút únfastened

Leaflet: Síngle sheet óf paper prínted ón each facets and fólded.

Jóúrnal: A bóók wíth blank pages ínteríór, tó let yóú wríte dówn any nón-públíc statístícs. Anóther wórd fór a newspaper ór símílar bóóklet.

Newsletter: A búlletín, leaflet, pamphlet, ór newspaper allótted tó a selected target aúdíence.

Newspaper: A ebóók óf númeróús pages públíshed wíth ínfórmatíón, spórts, facts, and advertísíng and marketíng. Newspapers can be písted and dístríbúted each day, weekly, mónthly, qúarterly, ór annúally.

Magazíne: A e-bóók wíth frónt and back paper cóvers, públíshed wíth ínfórmatíón and advertísíng and marketíng. Sóme magazínes are públíshed and allótted each week ór each mónth.

Pamphlet: Can be a leaflet, bóóklet ór saddle-stapled bóóklet.

Electróníc públíshíng

Maín artícle: Electróníc públíshíng

ÞÞÞ

2

Ínternet Map Vísúalízatíón

Electróníc públíshíng (addítíónally knówn as e-públíshíng ór dígítal públíshíng ór ón líne públíshíng) íncludes the dígítal e-bóók óf e-bóóks, vírtúal magazínes, and the develópment óf vírtúal líbraríes and catalógúes. Electróníc públíshíng has becóme cómmón. Ít ís alsó túrníng íntó nót únúsúal tó dístríbúte bóóks, magazínes, and newspapers tó cónsúmers thróúgh dígítal gadgets, by way óf ón líne resóúrces.

Módern cómpútíng and networkíng have revólútíónízed públíshíng.

Server rack, delíveríng statístícs tó ínqúíríes.

Cóntent kínds

Types óf bóók alsó can be prómínent by way óf cóntent materíal:

Bróchúre: an ínfórmatíve repórt made fór marketíng servíces ór pródúcts, nórmally wíthín the shape óf a pamphlet ór leaflet.

Tract: a nón secúlar ór pólítícal argúment wrítten vía óne character and desígned tó be dísbúrsed únfastened, nórmally ínsíde the fórm óf a gúíde ór pamphlet, bút nów and agaín lónger.

Mónógraph: a prótracted research bóóklet wrítten by óne índívídúal.

Únpúblíshed wórks

A wórk that has nó lónger góne thróúgh públícatíón, and as a cónseqúence ísn't nórmally tó be had tó the general públíc, ór fór qúótatíón ín schólarly ór felóny cóntexts, ís called an únpúblíshed wórk. Ín sóme cases únpúblíshed wórks are bróadly referred tó, ór círcúlated thróúgh casúal way.[7] An aúthór whó has nó lónger yet públíshed a wórk may alsó be referred tó as beíng únpúblíshed.

The fame óf beíng únpúblíshed has specífíc ímpórtance ínsíde the prísón cóntext, where ít ís able tó talk tó the nón-públícatíón óf prísón ópíníóns ín the Úníted States

Públícatíón Type

Types óf Públícatíón

The fóllówíng ís a líst úníqúe sórts óf públícatíóns tó whích yóú may póst yóúr wórk. By explóríng yóúr óptíóns yóú may decíde whích type óf públícatíón wóúld be hígh-qúalíty súítable ón yóúr súbmíssíóns.

- Self-bóóklet
- Letters tó the Edítór
- Newspapers & Públícatíóns wíth a Staff óf Wríters
- Líterary Magazínes
- Óther Types óf Magazínes
- Schólarly Jóúrnals
- Webzínes
- Bóóks
- E-e bóók
- Aúdíóbóók
- Vídeóbóók

There are dístínctíve sórts óf bóók públíshers, dependíng specífícally avaílable ón the market fór the e-bóók. Whíle we óften cónsíder "exchange" públíshers, fólks whó públísh the bóóks nórmally óbserved ín bóókstóres, there alsó are edúcatíónal públíshers, expert públíshers, and óf dírectíón, self-públíshíng servíces. Whether yóú aspíre tó be an wríter ór dream óf gettíng a prócess ín edítóríal, yóú shóúld realíze abóút the specíal fórms óf e bóók públíshers.

Trade Bóók Públíshers

Trade e bóók públíshers cóllect, edít, pródúce, póst, and prómóte the bóóks yóú are móst próbable tó lóók ín a bríck-and-mórtar bóókstóre. These are tradítíónal públíshers creatíng bóóks fór a patrón readershíp. Whíle the ínner córpóratíón systems and agency óf cónventíónal alternate públíshers range, each typícally públíshes bóóks ín a húge fórm óf códecs (hardcóver, change paperback, mass market paperback, e-bóóks, aúdíóbóóks), and a large chóíce óf tópícs and genres.

Nóte that a few trade bóók públíshers are cómpónents óf larger medía entítíes whích can addítíónally very ówn textbóók públíshers. Whíle there are many exchange públíshers ínsíde the Úníted States, the fóremóst ónes are knówn as "the Bíg Fíve" e bóók públíshers.

Bóók Packagers and Bóók Develópers

Bóók packagers are órganízatíóns specíalíze ín creatíng bóóks tó be públíshed belów the ímprínt óf a alternate wríter. Anóther manner tó stúdy ís that the públísher "óútsóúrces" the ímpróvement ín theír e-bóók. Ín persón públíshíng, packaged bóóks óften ínvólve a varíety óf phótógraphy ór example, and the públísher reveals ít greater fee-effectíve tó búy the bóóks already pródúced than tó bróaden and cónvey the vólúmes themselves. Sóme yóúnger persón fíctíón seríes alsó are packaged.

The e-bóók packager develóps an ídea fór a ebóók (ór cóllectíón óf bóóks) after whích sells the cóncept tó a wríter. The packager then dóes all óf the edítóríal and manúfactúríng paíntíngs fór the wríter (wíth públísher appróval at key júnctúres óf the manner) and cómmónly shíps the cómpleted bóóks dírectly tó the públísher's warehóúse.

Ín a few cases, the packager próvídes the dócúments, and the bóók wríter prínts and bínds the bóóks. Whíle the name óf the e-bóók packager ís nórmally únknówn tó the patrón shóppíng fór the e bóók, there may be typícally an íllústratíón óf the packager sómewhere ón the títle page.

The aúthórs óf packaged bóóks are cómmónly shrúnk as "paíntíngs fór rent;" thís ís, they're paíd a flat charge and dó nów nót get paíd róyaltíes ón the ebóók íncóme. An ínstance óf a bóók packager ís the San Franciscó-based Weldón Ówen.

"Bargaín" Bóók Públíshers

These públíshers create lów-valúe bóóks and e-bóók-related pródúcts (whích únclúde calendars ór actívíty kíts that encómpass bóóks) fór the "bargaín" segment óf the bóókshóp. The lów-príce nón-fíctíón bóóks are typícally íncredíbly íllústrated (sóúvenír bóóks, craft bóóks); the fíctíón cónsísts óf bínd-ú.S.A.Óf númeróús nóvels fróm a dístíngúíshed, prólífíc wríter ór reprínts óf classícs ínsíde the públíc dómaín. Sóme prómótíónal e-bóók públíshers alsó púrchase and re-sell the remaínders óf change bóóks.

Aúthórs whó wríte aúthentíc bóóks fór thís marketplace are nearly cónstantly shrúnk fór paíntíngs-fór-lease. Establíshed aúthórs whó are reprínted íntó thís market are dóíng só beneath reprínt claúses ín theír públíshíng cóntracts and acqúíre róyaltíes fór hís ór her wórk.

Textbóók Públíshers and Academíc Públíshers

Textbóók públíshers create bóóks fór facúlty and cóllege lectúre róóms, generally wíth a partícúlar cóúrse syllabús ín thóúghts. Schóól e-bóók públíshers are called "elhí," a cómbínatíón óf "símple" and "excessíve schóól."

The fóremóst textbóók públíshers are McGraw-Híll, Pearsón, Reed Elsevíer, and Hóúghtón Mífflín.

Prófessíónal Públíshers

Próféssíónal públíshers create bóóks and databases fór próféssíónals whó need get admíssíón tó tó relíable, wídely wídespread recórds and requírements. These cónsíst óf (bút are nót restraíned tó) accóúntants, archítects, medícal dóctórs, attórneys, and psychólógísts. Becaúse óf the qúantíty óf statístícs ín thóse bóóks and the want fór freqúently úpdated ínfórmatíón, a lót óf thís statístícs has móved fróm predómínantly bóók shape tó ón-líne get ríght óf entry tó. An ínstance óf a expert wríter ís Jóhn Wíley.

Self-Públíshíng Servíces

Ín trendy, self-públíshers, thróúgh any name, permít an wríter tó peer theír e bóók ín prínt ór ón-líne and handy tó an target aúdíence. Hówever, there are awesóme dífferences between "beíng públíshed" hístórícally and havíng yóúr bóók pródúced by úsíng a self-públíshíng próvíder.

That saíd, there are extraórdínary reasóns tó self-póst, bút regúlarly an wríter chóóses tó achíeve thís whíle hís ór her e-bóók's enchantment tó the óverall clíent ísn't óbvíóús enóúgh fór a tradítíónal exchange wríter tó take a threat ón ít. Whíle varíóús self-públíshers ór cónceítedness públíshers óffer specífíc tíers óf help wíth and help fór the públíshíng system, self-públíshíng servíces cóme at a rate, paíd fór wíth the aíd óf the aúthór.

Sóme self-públíshíng ófferíngs íncládé: Lúlú.Cóm, Barnes & Nóble's NÓÓK Press, Blúrb, and íÚníverse

Hybríd Públísher

Hybríd públíshers' ófferíngs fall sómewhere amóng a self-públíshíng agency and a tradítíónal públísher. Hybríd públíshers díffer sígnífícantly óf theír terms. Stíll, they úsúally óffer theír aúthórs a few degree óf ín-hóúse edítóríal ínfórmatíón and dístríbútíón aíd, and they share wíthín the íncóme that end resúlt fróm the e bóók sales. Sóme examples óf hybríd públíshers íncládé SheWrítes, Entangled, and Bóóktrópe.

E-bóók

Ít ís the cóntent that súbjects, nót the fórmat – whíle analyzíng ón e-ínk readers, tablets and smartphónes ís an vítal a part óf míllíóns' líves, there are nevertheless óther míllíóns whó wóúldn't ever take íntó accóúnt dównlóadíng a bóók. Despíte theír grówíng recógnítíón, there are nevertheless númeróús míscónceptíóns abóút ebóóks wórldwíde. Thís artícle targets tó óffer a amateúr's manúal tó fólks that nónetheless trúst that the smell óf ínk and paper ís an ímpórtant accessóry óf reading. What's an e-bóók? Read ón tó stúdy extra appróxímately epúb.

The artícle has been úpdated ón Janúary three, 2018 wíth módífícatíóns.

Bóók and e-bóók reader

1. What's an e-bóók?

Thís shóúld be hónest tó reply, yóú wóúld thínk. At fírst lóók, lets say that an ebóók ís a ebóók read ón an dígítal devíce (laptóp dísplay screen, píll, telephóne ór e-reader). Bút thís descríptíón ís sómewhat índístínct and wíde, íncludíng many thíngs that aren't an ebóók. Therefóre ít's far hígher tó methód thís qúery fróm the attítúde óf what's a dístínctíón amóng an epúb, a wórd recórd and a PDF recórd.

A) The text ís nót edítable

Whíle yóú may (and dó) read yóúr fríend's díssertatíón ór yóúr neíghbór's recípe e-bóók ín yóúr cellphóne, ít dóesn't rely as an ebóók as lóng as yóú may alternate the textúal cóntent. Ebóóks made fór públíc dístríbútíón are ín a layóút that ís nót smóóth tó trade (ídeally ímpóssíble) wíthóút the wríter's permíssíón. All ebóók readíng apps are desígned tó límít any sórt óf módífyíng even as leavíng ópen the óppórtúníty óf íncludíng nótes and híghlíghtíng (wíthóút cónvertíng the aúthentíc dócúment).

B) The textúal cóntent ís reflówable (úntíl ít ísn't)

While PDFs are literally impóssíble tó edít, they stíll dón't qúalífy as ebóóks: when yóú have ever attempted analyzíng a PDF ón a tíny dísplay screen, yóú flawlessly recógníse why. Yóú can't alternate the layóút: analyzíng a PDF ón an e-reader tóól ís nearly as úncómfórtable as phótógraphíng an entíre e-bóók and stúdyíng that (that ís sóme thíng nóne fólks míght ever dó, glaríngly). PDF ís the ríght layóút fór prínt: ít's far desígned wíth the exact paper length ín mínd. Ít always lóóks as íf the prínt módel. Never adjústments.

Ebóóks, ón the óther hand, are created ín a fórmat that adjústments shape cónsístent wíth the devíce yóú stúdy ít ón. Yóú wíll nevertheless have chapters and paragraphs, hówever the líne breaks aren't cómpelled: ít'll úsúally flawlessly fíll yóúr screen. Yóú cóúnt ón websítes alternate theír layóúts whíle yóú're lóókíng at them fróm yóúr píll ór cellphóne; the eqúal ís góíng fór epúbs.

The epúb 3 fashíónable, hówever, delívered fíxed-layóút epúbs: everythíng ón the dísplay screen has an absólúte róle. Fíxed-fórmat epúbs lóse lóts óf theír adaptabílíty hówever stíll realíze the devíce and app they're dísplayed wíth.

C) Yóú set yóúr very ówn regúlatíóns

Since the fórmat ísn't cónstant, yóú may be gíven the óptíón tó persónalíze ít and trade ít tó yóúr ówn needs: the detaíls flúctúate by devíce, bút yóú are cómmónly gíven múltíple fónts tó chóóse fróm (úsúally a seríf, a mónóspace and a sans-seríf) and may exchange fónt síze and líne spacíng. And we have nót even nóted splendíd húge prínt and text-tó-speech óppórtúnítíes móst e-readers ínclúde – ebóóks carry lóng awaíted ídentícal póssíbílítíes íntó readíng.

Whíle thóse are the basíc characterístícs, ebóóks can dó that and plenty extra: búílt ín díctíónaríes can assíst yóúr langúage stúdyíng, línks enable smóóth navígatíón between chapters and they have fírst-rate múltímedía capabílíty – móre súítable ebóóks are the súbject óf sóme óther artícle. They dón't smell líke tradítíónal bóóks, hówever they are smóóth tó carry róúnd, best fór óne-exceeded stúdyíng and líterally ímpóssíble tó lóse. (Well, yóú may lóse yóúr tóól, hówever Í'm súre everybódy cóntínúes agaín-úsaínsíde the clóúd.)

Nów ít's clean what's an e-bóók and what's nót. Let's see whó gót here úp wíth the ídea fírst!

Hístóry óf bóóks, líbrary

2. Hístóry

The cóncept óf a líbrary that fíts ón yóúr pócket has been ímagíned by way óf númeróús wríters óver the last centúry, bút by the póínt readers had been ínterested ín The Hítchhíker's Gúíde tó the Galaxy (1978), ebóóks have been already aróúnd.

The Prójeсt Gútenberg túrned íntó laúnched ín 1971, develóping ebóóks as we realíze them nówadays, and dígítalízíng bóóks ever síncе. We nónetheless had tó waít úntíl 1998 fór the fírst e-reader gadgets tó emerge (Rócket Ebóók and Sóftbóók), bút the leap fórward dídn't manífest tíll 2007, whíle Amazón laúnched theír very very ówn e-reader, Kíndle. Wíth the dramatíc príce dróp ín 2010, the óppósítíón amóng the maín pródúcers expanded (Kíndle, Kóbó and Nóók beíng the leaders óf the Western market) and the pópúlaríty óf ebóóks and e-readers skyrócketed.

Cúrrently, maxímúm ebóóks are óffered wíthín the ÚS and ÚK, bút dífferent markets alsó are grówíng theír market share: Chína, Germany and Japan are leadíng the líst.

Famóús devíces: e-bóók reader

three. Pópúlar devíces

What's an e-bóók tóól? Ebóóks may be stúdy ón any vírtúal dísplay screen: cómpúter systems, capsúles, íPads, smartphónes and e-readers. Tó make súre pórtabílíty, larger agencíes (whíchínclúdes Amazón and Kóbó) próvíde yóú wíth all-platfórm apps: yóú can start readíng tó yóúr cómpúter whíle drínkíng yóúr mórníng cóffee, keep whereín yóú left óff ín yóúr e-reader and end fór yóúr telephóne.

Sóme húman beíngs bear ín mínd thís stúpíd, hówever Í fínd ít charmíng: my e-reader gót here wíthóút cónstrúcted ín líghtíng, só Í can't úse ít ín bed after my cómpaníón has lóng past tó sleep, hówever can maíntaín ón stúdyíng ón my cellphóne (wíth níght tíme móde róbótícally ón). Ít's magíc!

Whíle the age óf cheap smartphónes and drúgs bróúght abóút a lówer ín prómótíng devóted ebóók readers, there are nevertheless mótíves why óne wóúld púrchase an e-reader ín place óf a píll: e-readers ínclúde a battery lastíng fór weeks, capabílíty tó shóp húndreds óf bóóks, paperlíke e-ínk shów and the 'seasíde ímpact': whílst LED ís síncerely únreadable ín dírect daylíght, e-ínk wórks ín raín and shíne. (Dón't take ít wíth yóú tó the bathe althóúgh.)

We are aímíng tó devóte a whóle artícle evalúatíng the maxímúm pópúlar e-readers cúrrently avaílable, hówever pópúlar fúnctíóns cónsíst óf textúal cóntent-tó-speech, óbserve-takíng póssíbílítíes, smóóth amassíng and sharíng óf cósts and backlíght.

E-bóók stúdyíng wíth espressó

Phótó by way óf Alíís Sínísalú ón Únsplash

fóúr. Leadíng ebóók códecs: what's an epúb?

There are dózens óf e-bóók códecs, hówever maxímúm óf ús Earthly mórtals wíll símplest meet a paír thróúghóút óúr lífetíme. Ebóók readers typícally select a selected fórmat hówever móst óf them wíll nevertheless receíve móre than óne códecs. The dífference amóng the fórmats ís especíally ín hów próperly they cópe wíth cónstant-fórmat and reflówable bóóks, íf they gúíde DRM (dígítal replíca safety), whether they assíst píx and múltímedía cóntent and what are theír preferred gadgets.

A) .Txt (Plaín Text)

Yóú dón't recógníse hów far a símple text layóút wíll take yóú. Beíng the maxímúm extensívely standard ebóók fórmat, txt can't dó sóme thíng bút súpply símple, reflówable text. Ít's a wínner.

B) .Azw and .Azw3 (Kíndle)

Kíndle's very persónal fórmat can qúíte a whóle lót dó the whóle lót yóú expect fróm ít tó dó. Ít súppórts reflówable and fíxed fórmat bóóks, handles DRM and ínteractívíty. The ónly backsíde beíng that ít's far símplest famílíar wíth the aíd óf Kíndle devíces and Kíndle apps.

C) .Epúb (epúb)

ePúb, beíng cúrrently after íts 0.33 maín replace, can dó the whóle thíng the Kíndle layóút can, bút ís móre líkely wídespread: líterally every devíce can take care óf ePúb – besídes Kíndles, óf díréctíón. All óld e-bóók readers receíve epúb 2 fórmat, and maxímúm new readers sóak úp epúb 3: the fórmat óf ínteractíve, cónstant-layóút bóóks. Epúb three fórmat helps embeddíng óf nót handíest píx and sóúnds, bút even vídeós. Textbóóks and ínteractíve yóúngsters's bóóks are úsúally made úsíng epúb 3. Epúb three alsó gíves glóbal langúage help: ít handles nón-latín scrípts líke Arabíc and Chínese resúltseasíly.

D) .Móbí (Móbípócket)

When Amazón laúnched Kíndle, móbí túrned íntó the prímary fórmat they úsed. Whíle ít had ón the gróúnds that been replaced by way óf azw, ít ís stíll híghly famóús. Móbís may be examíne by almóst any devíce, besídes Nóóks and Sóny Readers.

E) .Pdf (Pórtable Dócúment Fórmat)

Whíle technícally nów nót an e-bóók layóút, thís ís the óne móst peóple are acqúaínted wíth. Desígned fór príntíng and easy, platfórm neútral sharíng óf fíxed-fórmat fíles, ít ís nó marvel that reflówíng the textúal cóntent ís íntrícate. (Ít can be accómplíshed, thóúgh.) The massíve backsíde óf pdf ís that ít ísn't always cónventíónal vía any óf the maín e-bóók shóps.

Ebóók reader prógrams

Phótó vía Wíllíam Íven ón Únsplash

fíve. Creatíng an e-bóók

Íf yóú have gót wrítten a ebóók and wóúld lóve tó dístríbúte ít ín príncípal shóps, yóú'll need tó create an ebóók. There are several ways óf dóíng ít: yóú can cónvert ít yóúr self ínsíde the clóúd, ín yóúr laptóp úsíng an e-bóók edítór, ór lease sómeóne tó dó the cónversíón.

Íf yóú wríte and edít yóúr e-bóók ín Wórd (ór anóther fíle prócessór), yóú'll have tó pút tógether the manúscrípt fór ebóók cónversíón. Thís ís próper ín case yóú entrúst a próféssíónal, hówever ís an íncreasíng númber óf só íf makíng a decísíón tó cónvert yóúr ebóók yóúrself. Mícrósóft Wórd and Góógle Dócs, bút, úse a whólly exclúsíve system óf stylíng and fórmattíng a bóók than e-bóók edítórs: íf the twó gadget clashes, ít ís able tó bríng abóút paín, sweat and lóng hóúrs óf tróúbleshóótíng.

The maxímúm crúcíal recómmendatíón we are able tó cóme úp wíth ís símply the recómmendatíón óf ameríca Navy. The KÍSS precept (Keep ít símple, sílly!) ís óne óf the majór príncíples óf ebóók fórmattíng. As the e-bóók reader apps and gadgets stríp the bóóks fróm maxímúm fórmattíng, there may be rarely a mótíve fór takíng hóúrs selectíng dístínctíve fónts and cólóratíóns. There ís a hónest hazard that ít receíved't be dísplayed anyway. Úse styles fór fórmattíng, ín partícúlar headíngs: thóse may be úsed tó create yóúr table óf cóntents later. There ísn't any want tó manúally add a table óf cóntents wíth web page númbers – page númbers are únínterpretable ín case óf an epúb.

Check óút óúr e-bóók wrítíng apps masterpóst fór recómmendatíón ón selectíng the fírst-class únfastened and paíd e-bóók cónversíón sóftware prógram and e-bóók edítórs.

Best e-bóók wrítíng apps

6. Dównlóadíng, begínníng and analyzíng ebóóks

Íf yóú dón't very ówn an e-reader, yóú can nevertheless have the cómplete ereadíng experíence. There are lóts óf apps lettíng yóú búy, prepare, bórrów, lend and – móst ímpórtantly – read ebóóks.

Readíng ebóóks ón PC ór cómpúter (Wíndóws and Mac)

New Wíndóws cómpúters cóme wíth a búílt-ín answer fór ópeníng ebóóks: the Mícrósóft Edge brówser ís set as defaúlt fór cómmencíng epúb fíles. Whíle the manner ít shóws ít's míles never pretty, ít's míles súrely legíble.

By all means the maxímúm famóús sóftware tó ópen, examíne, órganíse and cónvert (fór prívate úse) ebóóks ón a laptóp ór laptóp pc ís Calíbre. Calíbre ís the nón-íncóme lóve ínfant óf Kóvíd Góyal and ís an ebóók dealíng wíth óúght tó-have. Ít ís way tó Calíbre that my e-bóók líbrary ís a góód deal hígher órganísed than my bódíly. Ít wórks líterally ón any platfórm: Mac, Línúx and Wíndóws. Calíbre dóes nó lónger best paíntíngs as an e-bóók reader, hówever cónverts the whóle lót tó everythíng, has a códe-based tótally edítór and ís fantastíc at metadata manager. Ít alsó can send bóóks tó the ebóók reader, even thróúgh e-maíl tó Kíndle. Í had fírst-rate úse óf thís capabílíty when Í labóred as a beta-reader: ít made cónvertíng phrase fíles fór nón-públíc úse a baby's play.

The tíme machíne (epúb)

Móst large dístríbútórs develóped theír pass-platfórm apps tó make súre synchrónísatíón, próper shów and prótectíón. Kíndle app wórks bóth fróm PC and Mac, and Kóbó has íts ówn app fór cómpúter systems.

The líbrary próvíder ÓverDríve makes úse óf Adóbe Dígítal Edítíóns fór PC and Mac. ADE, nó matter íts ímperfectíóns ís the enterpríse wellknówn devíce fór dísplayíng and wórkíng wíth cónstant-fórmat epúbs. Ít ís alsó fócúsíng ón accessíbílíty capabílítíes, wórkíng íntently cóllectívely wíth the wórkíng devíce's persónal accessíbílíty óptíóns. At the tíme óf wrítíng thís text, ADE ís at versíón range 4.7 – maxímúm óf the úpgradesínclúde plenty wanted búg fíxes.

Adóbe Dígítal Edítíóns

Tó resólve the extreme próblem óf what's góíng tó my e-bóók appear líke ón exclúsíve gadgets, Amazón has develóped the Kíndle Prevíewer. Ít ís free fór Wíndóws and Mac, and súppórts many dístínct dísplay screen sízes and edítíóns óf Kíndle gadgets.

Readíng ebóóks ón Andróíd

All Andróíd devíces cóme wíth a búílt-ín ebóók analyzíng tóól: Góógle Play Bóóks. Yóú can úse Góógle Play bóóks tó read yóúr very ówn ebóóks íf they are ín an epúb ór pdf layóút. Yóú alsó can púrchase ebóóks wíthín the Góógle Play Bóóks keep.

Góógle Play

Úse the 'Úplóad dócúments' characterístíc fróm yóúr brówser tó úplóad bóóks íntó yóúr Góógle Play Bóóks accóúnt. Yóú can then reach them fróm yóúr phóne ór yóúr tablet.

Óther famóús apps encómpass Kíndle, Nóók and Kóbó, all wíth cónstrúcted ín shópping featúre. The líbrary gíant ÓverDríve úses Líbby fór telephónes and dífferent pórtable devíces. All óf these apps are capable óf handle nótes, híghlíghts ín úníqúe húes, maxímúm óf them have búílt-ín díctíónary, can manage categóríes ór shelves.

Readíng ebóóks ón íPhóne

The ídentícal ís real fór ÍÓS gadgets: all móst ímpórtant shóps have an ÍÓS well matched app, and só dóes Apple ítself. As bóóks pósted vía íTúnes are óf the very best hígh-qúalíty (Apple beíng óne óf the few dístríbútórs ín realíty reqúíríng a legítímate epúb), só anyóne stúdyíng bóóks bóúght díectly fróm Apple may be certaín that the bóóks are rúnníng ón the Apple devíce.

What ís an ebóók

Phótó by úsíng Alejandró Escamílla ón Únsplash

7. Dównlóad ebóóks

Yes, all óf ús realíze, ebóóks are extremely góód, bút whereín are yóú able tó get them fróm? Well, there are plenty óf servíces presentíng lóóse (felóny) ebóóks tó dówn lóad fór any platfórm. The pópúlar ónes encómpass Góógle Play bóók shóp, Próject Gútenbergand BóókBóón. Check óút thís lístíng fór greater.

Ít míght cómes as a wónder, hówever ít ís wórth sórtíng óút yóúr nearby líbrary: they'll ín all líkelíhóód have a agreement wíth a líbrary e-ebóók dealer. The Rakúten ówned ÓverDríve ís ín cóntract wíth 10.000 públíc and ínstítútíónal líbraríes wórldwíde, ín the maín ínsíde the ÚS, Canada, ÚK, bút addítíónally ín Brazíl, Índía and Nórway. Ín Chína, CNPeReadíng resóúrces líbraríes wíth sparklíng dígítal cóntent materíal. Móst próvíders ímpartíng thís carríer have a reachable and clean tó apply app: símply lóók fór yóúr desíred e-bóók ór aúdíóbóók straíght fróm yóúr telephóne.

Móst e-readers and apps allów yóú tó stóre and dównlóad ímmedíately fróm the platfórm, só that yóú receíved't óúght tó wórry appróxímately changíng. Íf yóú examíne a lót, yóú wóúld póssíbly want tó keep ín mínd sígníng as múch as a súbscríptíón carríer,ínclúdíng Kíndle Únlímíted, Bóókmate ór Scríbd.

Have yóú wrítten an ebóók? Ór are yóú pretty múch tó wríte óne? Íf yóú want assíst wíth módífyíng, cónversíón ór dístríbútíón, dó nót hesítate tó cóntact ús – we're ríght here tó help.

Púrchasíng eBóóks

There are lóts óf óútlets that yóú cóúld púrchase eBóóks fróm. Sóme óf the móst cómmón, eReader-líke mínded óútletsínclúde Amazón, Barnes & Nóble, Kóbó, and Góógle Play. Yóú alsó can cróss dírectly tó a órganísatíón ór wríter's ínternet síte – óftentímes, aúthórs wíll sell theír eBóók ón theír very ówn websíte ónlíne.

Benefíts óf eBóóks

Wíth eBóóks delívered tó the arena óf stúdyíng, have yóú ever ever púzzled what óúght tó próbably make them hígher than tradítíónal paperback bóóks? Í even have, and ríght here are ónly a few óf the blessíngs óf eBóóks:

eBóóks keep space

Sóme húmans are fórtúnate súffícíent tó have húge líbraríes tó keep theír bóóks. Bút fór the bóókwórms whó dón't have that extra róóm, eBóóks shóp a terrífíc qúantíty óf area by úsíng permíttíng readers tó keep lóts óf bóóks ón óne tóól. Nó extra attemptíng tó fínd space tó shóp yóúr new bóóks.

EBóóks stóre cash

Í knów thís óne caúght yóúr eye, becaúse whó dóesn't want tó stóre cash? Wíth nó manúfactúríng ór shíppíng cósts, eBóóks are cheaper than paperback bóóks. The cómmón rate óf an eBóók earríngs ín at less than $fíve, whereas paperback bóóks are generally greater than $10. Míght nów nót appear líke a great deal, bút ít adds úp íf yóú're an avíd reader.

EBóóks save the envírónment

Qúíte ín all líkelíhóód my favóríte gaín óf eBóóks. The e-bóók-príntíng enterpríse cónsúmes 16 míllíón lóts óf paper each 12 mónths; that's 32 míllíón trees. And dón't get me started ón the amóúnt óf póllútants that factóríes laúnch íntó the aír. Talk abóút an large carbón fóótprínt.

Wíth eBóóks makíng úp róúnd 30 percentage óf e-bóók íncóme, they nó lónger móst effectíve keep strength and decrease póllútíón, bút addítíónally they keep abóút 9.6 míllíón óf thóse 32 míllíón trees yearly! A wín fór anybódy.

EBóóks are pórtable and cónveníent

Anythíng that makes lífe less cómplícated fór húman beíngs ís appealíng, and cómfórt ís a real crówd pleaser. EBóóks are pórtable AND cónveníent. Wíth a súppórted eBóók devíce, yóú can have a líbrary at yóúr fíngertíps. Carryíng róúnd yóúr preferred bóóks ín yóúr íPad, eReader, phóne, ór table (all líght-weíght devíces!) sóúnds plenty less díffícúlt than lúggíng róúnd óne thóúsand paperback bóóks ín case yóú ask me.

Ínstantly dównlóad eBóóks

Nówadays, whílst húmans want sóme thíng, they need ít nów. Yóú can púrchase an eBóók fróm vírtúally everywhere ón any eBóók súppórted devíce wíth the cóntact óf a búttón and dównlóad ít ríght away. Nó extra úsíng tó the stóre and wanderíng aróúnd fór hóúrs shúfflíng thrú the dózens óf bóókshelves ór watchíng fór yóúr órder tó arríve. Yóú can effórtlessly get entry tó eBóóks every tíme and anywhere, and begín stúdyíng ríght away.

Yóú can trade the fónt síze óf an eBóók

Dependíng at the fórmat (exclúdes PDF), yóú may trade the fónt síze óf an eBóók. Thís ís maínly attractíve tó the ónes whó've a dífficúlt tíme seeíng. Nó extra sqúíntíng ór accómplíshíng ín yóúr glasses. Ít's best and easy tó cústómíze yóúr fónt síze wíth an eBóók.

Althóúgh yóú may't alternate the fónt length óf a PDF eBóók, yóú cóntínúe tó can zóóm ín tó yóúr devíce. Nót as handy, bút nevertheless sóme thíng yóú cóúld't dó wíth a paperback bóók.

EBóóks are searchable

Únlíke paperback bóóks, eBóóks are wíthóút dífficúlty searchable. Ínstead óf flíppíng thróúgh the pages attemptíng tó fínd a favóríte qúóte ór a part óf the stóry, yóú cóúld móve lówer back wíth the aíd óf lóókíng keywórds tó díscóver the phase óf yóúr bóók yóú had been searchíng óút. Thís ís partícúlarly benefícíal when yóú're readíng lengthy bóóks that míght take hóúrs tó flíp thróúgh searchíng óút a partícúlar page.

What ís an e-bóók

Why create an eBóók?

Íf yóú're thínkíng abóút makíng an eBóók, ít's maxímúm próbable fór cónsídered óne óf reasóns:

Self-bóók púrpóses

As part óf yóúr advertísíng appróach

Whatever the case can be, let's stúdy why yóú have tó círcúlate fórward wíth makíng an eBóók.

Self-Públícatíón

Whether ít's a research paper ór clearly a e-bóók yóú've been wórkíng ón, self-públíshíng an eBóók ís a hígh-qúalíty cóncept fór everybódy lóókíng tó share theír thóúghts wíth the arena. Nót certaín the way tó súbmít an eBóók? Dón't allów that stand ín yóúr manner; ít ís pretty easy and really wórth the effórt. Gíven the fact that eBóóks are shareable and wíthóút próblems reachable tó readers, new wríters can amplífy theír aúdíence thróúgh sharíng theír eBóóks ón líne.

They're addítíónally a fantastíc way tó advantage self assúrance tó yóúr partícúlar cóncern matter and enhance yóúr wrítíng abíltíes. Creatíng an eBóók tó edúcate readers permíts yóú tó amplífy yóúr expertíse ón the tópíc, establísh yóúr ínfórmatíón, and develóp yóúr wrítíng and módífyíng cómpetencíes alóngsíde the way.

Marketíng Strategy

eBóóks are gettíng an íncreasíng númber óf pópúlar as a part óf advertísíng strategíes. Thís ís dúe tó the fact cóntent materíal ís the spíne óf ínbóúnd advertísíng and marketíng, and the qúalíty óf that cóntent can make ór wreck an ínbóúnd advertísíng strategy. When ít cómes tó stúdyíng yóúr methód, knów-hów what fórm óf cóntent wórks fírst-class ín each stage wíll assíst yóú súccessfúlly plan yóúr ínbóúnd marketíng strategy.

EBóóks are maínly terrífíc assets wíthín the attract degree óf the ínbóúnd advertísíng appróach. They create emblem advertísíng fócús and próvíde cóst tó vísítórs (abílíty cústómers) thróúgh gívíng them sóme thíng that ís benefícíal tó them. Íf yóú manípúlate tó dó ít próper, yóú may túrn thóse traffíc íntó leads vía gatheríng theír tóúch detaíls and móvíng them tó the cónvert level.

As a marketer, wrítíng an eBóók ís a fantastíc óppórtúníty tó be the óne-stóp keep that readers want. Wíth ínfórmatíve, treasúred cóntent, yóú'll appeal tó strangers ón yóúr websíte and óffer yóúr enterpríse wíth capabílíty leads. Hów dó these síte vísítórs end úp leads, yóú ask? Íf yóú cóllect theír tóúch facts, alóng wíth theír emaíl addresses. A fírst-rate example óf hów pówerfúl eBóóks may be ín yóúr advertísíng effórts.

Hów tó make an eBóók

Ít can be óverwhelmíng stúdyíng the way tó make an eBóók, hówever they're certaínly pretty smóóth tó pút tógether and prómóte wíth a bít steeríng.

The prócedúre starts wíth defíníng yóúr óbjectíves and aúdíence. Why are yóú wrítíng the eBóók and whó are yóú wrítíng ít fór? Knówíng these ítems wíll then wíll let yóú chóóse a súbject wíth a víew tó nót móst effectíve hóbby yóúr target market, bút addítíónally satísfy the púrpóse yóú're wrítíng the eBóók ín the fírst area.

Ónce yóú've selected a súbject, píck a specífíc títle tó púlls ón yóúr readers. Ít shóúld addítíónally gíve them a púrpóse tó want tó examíne yóúr eBóók; a índístínct títle wón't get yóú very a lóng way.

Fróm there, begín óútlíníng yóúr eBóók thróúgh makíng plans an pówerfúl íntródúctíón, breakíng yóúr eBóók íntó chapters, and planníng súítable calls-tó-móvement placements dúríng the eBóók. Creatíng thís óútlíne wíll save yóú tíme after yóú begín wrítíng.

Wrítíng yóúr eBóók need tó be fún. Thís ís yóúr hazard tó reveal readers that yóú're an próféssíónal ón the cóncern yóú're wrítíng appróxímately.Ínclúde detaíls, be creatíve, and dísplay them what yóú're fabrícated fróm. Be pósítíve tó próófread ónce yóú're achíeved!

Next cómes the layóút. Fróm cólóúr tó vísúals tó brandíng and fónt, the desígn óf yóúr eBóók have tó cómplement the cóntent ít'll cónsíst óf. Yóúr títle shóúld púll the reader ín, bút the layóút múst help wíth that tóó.

Tó make yóúr eBóók seem smóóth tó read, recóllect the fórmattíng tóó; splít bíg blócks óf textúal cóntent wíth lísts and vísúals.

Fínally, yóú'll want tó transfórm, pút úp, and prómóte yóúr eBóók! Yóú've placed lóts óf thóúght íntó ít, ín addítíón tó ínvested a númber óf tíme ín ít. Só prómótíng ít's míles an essentíal step. Yóú need tó make certaín yóúr eBóók ís seen and stúdy. Creatíng a tóúchdówn page, the úse óf sócíal medía advertísíng, and íncórpóratíng yóúr eBóók tó yóúr blóg methód are all easy, yet pówerfúl, appróaches tó start prómótíng yóúr eBóók ríght away.

Types óf E-bóóks

Móre húman beíngs are analyzíng ebóóks than ever befóre. Theír decrease príce and móre pórtable natúre manner that they nów accóúnt fór 30 percent óf all e bóók sales ínsíde the Úníted States.

Ebóók-fórmats

Bút ít's nó lónger all exact ínfórmatíón fór clíents. Únlíke MP3s, whích yóú cóúld thrów óntó any sóng partícípant and cóúnt ón them tó paíntíngs, ebóóks are a maze óf própríetary and ópen fashíónable fórmats. Tó cómplícate matters fúrther, nów nót all e-readers assíst all códecs.

Ín thís newsletter, we lóók at a númber óf the móst cómmón códecs, próvíde an explanatíón fór theír prós and cóns, and tell yóú whích readers gúíde them.

1. EPÚB

EPÚB ís the maxímúm bróadly fóllówed e-bóók dócúment layóút. Ínítíally devélóped thróúgh the Ínternatíónal Dígítal Públíshíng Fórúm (that ís nów part óf the Wórld Wíde Web Cónsórtíúm), ít óútmóded the óld Ópen e-bóók fórmat (ÓEB) ín 2007.

Becaúse EPÚB ís únfastened tó apply, ópen preferred, and seller-índependent, ít has grówn tó end úp the móst cómmón ebóók layóút. Althóúgh nót óften seen, ít cóúld even assíst cólóúr píc s, SVG snap shóts, ínteractíve factórs, and cómplete vídeós.

Ín many methóds, ít ís the ebóók eqúal óf the trústy MP3---bóth ín a terrífíc and bad manner. Almóst all maínstream e-readers and pc wórkíng systems help the layóút, bút públíshers alsó can wrap ít ín any DRM system ín theír selectíng (even thóúgh yóú may dó away wíth the DRM ón any e-bóók yóú ówn).

Cast óff-drm-bóóks

Hów tó Remóve the DRM ón Every Ebóók Yóú Ówn

Nó óne líkes DRM. We all únderstand why ít exísts, hówever that dóesn't ímply we are prepared tó embrace ít. Therefóre, thís newsletter explaíns the way tó take away the DRM fróm every eBóók yóú ówn.

And the dísadvantage? Amazón Kíndle gadgets can nót read ít (besídes fór the Kíndle Fíre tablet). Íf yóú have a e-bóók ín the EPÚB fórmat whích yóú need tó stúdy tó yóúr Kíndle, yóú may cónvert ebóóks ríght íntó a óne óf a kínd fórmat the úsage óf Calíbre.

2. MÓBÍ

Líke EPÚB, the MÓBÍ layóút alsó grew óút óf the antíqúe ÓEB layóút. French emplóyer Móbípócket fórked ít ín 2000 and ít went ón tó fórm the premíse óf íts Móbípócket Reader sóftware prógram.

Amazón bóúght the órganísatíón ín 2005 and allówed ít tó flóúrísh fór 11 years. Ín Óctóber 2016, Amazón eventúally clóse dówn Móbípócket's ínternet síte and servers, hówever the MÓBÍ layóút maíntaíns tó líve ón.

There are sóme key varíatíóns amóng EPÚB and MÓBÍ. Móst pertínently, ít ísn't ópen wídespread and, cónseqúently, ís nót públícly avaílable. Ít alsó can nót aíd sóúnd ór vídeó.

Ónce ónce móre, íts súppórted wíth the aíd óf all óf the ímpórtant e-readers wíth óne exceptíón: the Barnes and Nóble Nóók.

Nóte: The MÓBÍ fórmat alsó úses the PRC extensíón.

3. AZW And AZW3

The AZW and AZW3 extensíóns are Amazón's twó próprí etary ebóók fórmats. AZW ís the ólder óf the 2; ít debúted alóng the prímary Kíndle agaín ín 2007. AZW3 arríved ín 2011 wíth the díscharge óf the Kíndle Fíre reader.

Whenever yóú búy ór dównlóad an ebóók fróm Amazón, yóú'll get hóld óf ít ón yóúr devíce ín óne óf the twó códecs. AZW3 ís extra súperíór than AZW. Ít súppórts greater styles, fónts, and layóúts.

Behínd the scenes, each fórmats are extraórdínaríly símílar tó the MÓBÍ fórmat. Althóúgh ít's never been públícly shówed, ít's extensívely assúmed that the reasón Amazón óffered Móbípócket was só ít can úse the únderlyíng era as the basís fór íts AZW fórmat. Únlíke MÓBÍ, the Amazón fórmats each gúíde vídeó and sóúnd.

Becaúse AZW ís própríetary, ít ísn't as bróadly súppórted ón e-readers as EPÚB and MÓBÍ. Natúrally, all óf Amazón's Kíndle merchandíse can stúdy the layóút, hówever dífferent famóús gadgets cónsístíng óf the Nóók and Kóbó e-readers cannót.

Andróíd and íÓS can bóth examíne AWZ, and ít ís alsó readable ón famóús e-bóók cóntról apps líke Calíbre and Alfa.

4. ÍBA

The óther cómmónplace próprietary ebóók fórmat that yóú're próbable tó stúmble thróúghóút ís ÍBA. Ít ís the layóút úsed fór bóóks created ín Apple's íBóóks Aúthór app.

Technícally, the layóút cóúld be very símílar tó EPÚB. Hówever, ít ís based ón cústóm wídget códe wíthín the Apple Bóóks app tó fúnctíón and cónseqúently can't be úníversally stúdy ón all e-readers.

Remember, thís layóút ís ónly úsed fór bóóks wrítten ín íBóóks Aúthór. Íf yóú búy regúlar great-sellíng ebóóks fróm the íTúnes save, they'll be delívered ínsíde the EPÚB fórmat (thóúgh they may be DRM-restrícted).

The íBóók layóút súppórts vídeó, sóúnd, píçs, and ínteractíve elements.

5. PDF

The últímate fóremóst ebóók layóút ín móvement ís PDF. Becaúse óf the layóút's góód sízed adóptíón aróúnd the net, PDFs have túrn óút tó be a pópúlar way óf delíveríng ebóóks.

Íts large drawback ís the lack óf natíve reflówíng. Reflówíng ís the tíme períód úsed tó explaín whíle a fíle can adapt íts presentatíón ín líne wíth the dímensíóns óf the screen ór the settíngs a persón decíded ón.

All the devóted ebóók fórmats óffer reflówíng prímaríly based at the seqúence óf óbjects wíthín the cóntent materíal-stream. The PDF layóút can círcúmnavígate the lack óf órdínary reflówíng vía the úse óf tags tó óútlíne the únderlyíng shape óf a dócúment. Hówever, tagged PDFs are nónetheless nót well súppórted wíth the aíd óf ebóók readers.

Ón the súperb síde, ít ís best the secónd layóút at the líst thís ís ópen preferred; ít became ÍSÓ 32000 agaín ín 2008.

Óther Ebóók Fórmats Tó Be Aware Óf

There are sóme less-nót únúsúal fórmats yóú míght see fróm tíme-tó-tíme...

6. LRS, LRF, And LRX

LRS, LRF, and LRX are the repórt extensíóns fór the Bróad Band ebóók fórmat. They had been próprietary fórmats that Sóny created tó be úsed ón íts persónal varíety óf ebóók readers.

LRS ís nów ópen fashíónable, hówever LRF and LRX stay clósed. Regardless, Sóny has deserted all 3 fórmats ín favór óf EPÚB.

7. FB2

The XML-based FB2 began exístence ín Rússía. Ít ís nót únúsúal amóng e-bóók cóllectórs thanks tó íts capacíty tó keep metadata wíthín the e-bóók recórd ítself.

Ít addítíónally clósely úsed as a stórage fórmat dúe tó the ease wíth whích ít ís able tó be cónverted íntó dífferent códecs.

Eíght. DJVÚ

DJVÚ ís famóús ín the medícal cómmúníty. Ít bóasts a cómpressíón thís ís abóút 10 ínstances hígher than PDF; ít cóúld keep extra than a húndred black and whíte scans ín less than a megabyte.

Nóte: Yóú can redúce the scale óf a PDF wíth a few cómpressíón hínts.

Níne. LÍT

LÍT changed íntó Mícrósóft's própríetary ebóók layóút. When DRM-enabled, the bóóks have been best readable at the Mícrósóft Reader app.

Ín 2011, Mícrósóft díscóntínúed the LÍT fórmat. Reader vaníshed earlíer thís 12 mónths.

10. RFT

The Rích Text Fórmat ís líke mínded wíth each e-reader ón the market. Ít has an advantage óver TXT becaúse óf íts capacíty tó maíntaín specíal characters and íts aíd fór reflówíng and text fórmattíng.

EPÚB Vs. MÓBÍ Vs. AZW: Whích Óne Ís Best?

Ín fact, the handíest fórmats yóú need tó fear abóút are EPÚB, MÓBÍ, and AZW.

Íf yóú íntend ón cónstrúctíng a cónsíderable ebóók líbrary ín yóúr laptóp ít ís súppórted ón móst readers, stay wíth EPÚB. Íf yóú need tó create a líbrary ít's predómínately Kíndle-úníqúe, chóóse MÓBÍ. Ít dóes nót have pretty as many capabílítíes as AZW hówever greater devíces can stúdy ít.

ᑭᑭᑭ

Aúdíó book

Aúdíóbóóks are vóíce recórdíngs óf the text óf a e-bóók that yóú pay attentíón tó rather than examíne. Aúdíóbóóks can be precíse wórd-fór-phrase varíatíóns óf bóóks ór abrídged varíatíóns. Yóú can lísten tó aúdíóbóóks ón any phóne, píll, laptóp, dómestíc speaker devíce, ór ín-car enjóyment system.

Aúdíóbóóks are cómmónly púrchased and dównlóaded ínsíde the same manner as dígítal sóng and vídeó. They can alsó be bóúght fróm ónlíne bóókstóres ór dównlóaded únfastened fróm públíc area sítes. Móst públíc líbrary systems óffer aúdíóbóók dównlóads ón líne—all yóú need ís a líbrary card. Even Spótífy has an aúdíóbóók segment.

Fínd Óút the Best Websítes fór Dównlóadíng Free Aúdíó Bóóks

Hów Dó Yóú Lísten tó an Aúdíóbóók?

Avaílable as vírtúal aúdíó fíles, aúdíóbóóks may be perfórmed ón a extensíve type óf cónsúmer dígítal devíces, whích înclúde telephónes, drúgs, and cómpúter systems—any tóól that helps streamíng aúdíó..

When yóú púrchase ór dówn lóad aúdíóbóóks fróm the net, they cómmónly are avaílable óne óf the fóllówíng aúdíó fórmats:

MP3

WMA (Wíndóws Medía Aúdíó)

AAC (Advanced Aúdíó Códíng)

Móst medía gadgets are desígned tó play any óf these dócúment types.

There are many web sítes and apps that óffer get entry tó tó aúdíóbóóks, bóth free and paíd. Here are a few them:.

Apple Bóóks: Aúdíóbóóks fór íÓS and macÓS devíces are tó be had fór dównlóad at the Apple Bóóks app and save.

Aúdíble.Cóm: Whíle aúdíóbóóks can be bóught índívídúally, Aúdíble gíves a mónth-tó-mónth súbscríptíón servíce that próvídes óne lóóse aúdíóbóók dówn lóad per mónth. Úse the Aúdíble app fór Andróíd ór íÓS tó cóncentrate ón cellúlar gadgets.

AllYóúCanBóóks.Cóm: Thís websíte ónlíne óffers límítless access tó heaps óf dównlóadable aúdíóbóóks. Thís paíd websíte gíves the fírst mónth wíthóút spendíng a díme.

Próject Gútenberg: Thís web page ís famóús fór súpplyíng húndreds óf free bóóks ín the públíc dómaín. Nót as wídely knówn ís íts grówíng seríes óf húman-read aúdíóbóóks that may be accessed óver the ínternet.

Dównpóúr: A índústríal aúdíóbóók web síte that sells índívídúal aúdíóbóóks ín addítíón tó a mónthly súbscríptíón, ín case yóú'd ópt fór.

Nóók Aúdíóbóóks: Barnes & Nóble's aúdíóbóók ínternet síte sells a bíg seríes óf aúdíóbóóks.

ÓverDríve: An app that óffers heaps óf aúdíóbóóks fróm greater than 30,000 lócal líbraríes.

Hístóry óf Aúdíóbóóks

Aúdíóbóóks can be dated lówer back tó the Thírtíes. They had been freqúently úsed as an edúcatíónal medíúm, díscóvered ín schóóls and líbraríes. Befóre aúdíóbóóks were avaílable dígítally, speakíng bóóks, as they were óften nóted, have been sóld ín physícal fórm ón analóg cassette tapes and vínyl recórds. Hówever, wíth the ínventíón óf the net, a tremendóús selectíón óf aúdíóbóóks had been avaílable fróm many specífíc assets.

Types óf Aúdíó Bóók

Aúdíó dócúments cóme ín all kínds and sízes. And the móst nót únúsúal aúdíóbóók códecs may be dówn íntó twó majór categóríes: lóssless cómpressed aúdíó códecs and lóssy cómpressed aúdíó códecs. Móst óf yóú may be acqúaínted wíth MP3 layóút, what appróxímately óther fórmats, líke AAC, FLAC ór WMA? Whích ónes need tó yóú care abóút and whích ónes are yóú able tó fórget abóút?

- 1. Lóssy Cómpressed Aúdíó Fórmats
- 2. Lóssless Cómpressed Aúdíó Fórmats

1. Lóssy Cómpressed Aúdíó Fórmats

Lóssy cómpressíón ís a fórm óf cómpressíón that lóses recórds ín the cóúrse óf the cómpressíón prócess. Ín the cóntext óf aúdíó, whích means sacrífícíng níce and cónstancy fór fíle length. The excellent ínfórmatíón ís that, ín maxímúm ínstances, yóú míght nót be capable óf pay attentíón the dístínctíón.

MP3 (.Mp3)

MP3 ís the call óf the repórt extensíón and addítíónally the call óf the sórt óf repórt fór MPEG, aúdíó layer 3. Layer three ís óne óf three códíng schemes (layer 1, layer 2 and layer three) fór the cómpressíón óf aúdíó sígnals. Layer 3 makes úse óf perceptúal aúdíó códíng and psychó acóústíc cómpressíón tó dó away wíth all súperflúóús statístícs (extra especíally, the redúndant and írrelevant elements óf a valíd sígn. The stúff the húman ear dóes nót hear besídes). Ít alsó próvídes a MDCT (Módífíed Díscrete Cósíne Transfórm) that ímplements a fílter bank, íncreasíng the freqúency resólútíón 18 tímes hígher than that óf layer 2. The bríng abóút real terms ís layer 3 shrínks the úníqúe sóúnd ínfórmatíón fróm a CD (wíth a chúnk príce óf 1411.2 kílóbíts ín keepíng wíth óne 2nd óf stereó track) by means óf a element óf 12 (all the way dówn tó 112-128kbps) wíthóút sacrífícíng sóúnd satísfactóry.

AAX(.Aax)

Aúdíóbóók fórmat, whích ís a varíable-bítrate (allówíng hígh fíne) M4B recórd encrypted wíth DRM. M4B cónsísts óf AAC ór ALAC encóded aúdíó ín an MPEG-4 cóntaíner.

AAX recórd layóút ís created by means óf Aúdíble. Generally, AAX dócúments are encóded vía DRM and yóú may símplest cóncentrate tó Aúdíble aúdíóbóóks ón assígned sóftware prógram. Bút wíth the help óf Aúdíble Cónverter, yóú cóúld Cónvert Aúdíble Aúdíóbóók AAX tó MP3 tó yóúr favóríte aúdíó gamers ór sóme óther 0.33-party túne apps.

M4A/M4B(.M4a/.M4b)

M4A, an aúdíó-símplest MPEG-fóúr recórd, útílízed by Apple fór únprótected track dównlóaded fróm theír

íTúnes Músíc Stóre. Aúdíó ínsíde the m4a repórt ís nórmally encóded wíth AAC, althóúgh lóssless ALAC can alsó be úsed.

M4B, Aúdíóbóók/pódcast extensíón wíth AAC ór ALAC encóded aúdíó ín an MPEG-4 bóx. Bóth M4A and M4B códecs can cóntaín metadata tógether wíth chapter markers, píx, and línks, hówever M4B lets ín "bóókmarks", whíle M4A dóes nó lónger.

AAC(.Aac)

AAC stands fór Advanced Aúdíó Códíng. Ít changed íntó develóped ín 1997 as the súccessór tó MP3, and whílst ít díd captúre ón as a pópúlar layóút tó apply, ít never absólútely óvertóók MP3 becaúse the móst famóús fór órdínary músíc and recórdíng.

The cómpressíón algóríthm úsed by AAC ís an awfúl lót extra súperíór and technícal than MP3, só whíle yóú examíne a partícúlar recórdíng ín MP3 and AAC códecs at the eqúal bítrate, the AAC óne wíll typícally have better sóúnd great.

Agaín, despíte the fact that MP3 ís móre óf a hóúsehóld layóút, AAC ís extensívely úsed nówadays. Ín trúth, ít ís the úsúal aúdíó cómpressíón appróach úsed by YóúTúbe, Andróíd, íÓS, íTúnes, later Níntendó pórtables, and later PlayStatíóns.

M4P (.M4p)

A módel óf AAC wíth própríetary Dígítal Ríghts Management(Faírplay DRM) develóped by Apple fór úse ín sóng dównlóaded fróm theír íTúnes Músíc Stóre. M4P stands fór MPEG fóúr Prótected (aúdíó), that's a lóssy cómpressíón nórmally súppósed as the súccessór tó MP3. Ín trendy, M4P pródúces hígher sóúnd hígh-qúalíty and fíles óf smaller length, whílst ín cómparísón tó the MP3 fórmat.

Ógg (.Ógg)

ÓGG dóes nót stand fór sóme thíng. Actúally, ít ís nót even a cómpressíón fórmat. ÓGG ís a múltímedía cóntaíner whích can keep all types óf cómpressíón códecs, bút ís maxímúm cómmónly úsed tó preserve Vórbís dócúments — as a resúlt why these aúdíó fíles are knówn as Ógg Vórbís fíles.

Vórbís became fírst released ín 2000 and grew ín pópúlaríty dúe tó twó mótíves: fírst, ít adheres tó the ídeas óf ópen súpply sóftware, and 2d, ít plays sígnífícantly hígher than móst óther lóssy cómpressíón fórmats (í.E. Pródúces a smaller recórd length fór eqúal aúdíó satísfactóry).

MP3 and AAC have súch stúrdy fóóthólds that ÓGG has had a díffícúlt tíme breakíng íntó the híghlíght — nót many gadgets aíd ít natívely — bút ít's gettíng better wíth tíme. Fór nów, ít ís prímaríly úsed by hardcóre própónents óf ópen sóftware prógram.

WMA(.Wma)

WMA stands fór Wíndóws Medía Aúdíó. Ít túrned íntó fírst released ín 1999 and has góne thrú several evólútíón ón the gróúnds that then, all whíle retaíníng the ídentícal WMA name and extensíón. As yóú may assúme, ít's a própríetary fórmat created by úsíng Mícrósóft.

Nót ín cóntrast tó AAC and ÓGG, WMA changed íntó súppósed tó deal wíth sóme óf the faílíngs wíthín the MP3 cómpressíón techníqúe — and as súch, WMA's techníqúe tó cómpressíón ís pretty símílar tó AAC and ÓGG. Ín dífferent wórds, ín terms óf óbjectíve best, WMA ís hígher than MP3.

Bút cónsídering that WMA ís própríetary, nót many devíces and platfórms aíd ít. Ít alsó dóesn't óffer any actúal benefíts óver AAC ór ÓGG, só ín maxímúm ínstances whílst MP3 ís nót próper súffícíent, ít ís absólútely extra realístíc tó gó tógether wíth óne óf thóse twó ínstead.

2. Lóssless Cómpressed Aúdíó Fórmats

Ón the óther síde óf the cóín ís lóssless cómpressíón, that's a methód that redúces repórt síze wíthóút any lóss ín best between the úníqúe sóúrce dócúment and the ensúíng repórt. The dównsíde ís that lóssless cómpressíón ís nót as green as lóssy cómpressíón, meaníng eqúal dócúments can be 2x tó 5x large.

Thís ís manífestly a whóle lót móre díffícúlt tó dó próperly, bút there are a few córrect fórmats fór thís. And dón't cónfúse lóssless cómpressíón wíth excessíve-resólútíón aúdíó (whích ís maxímúm ín all líkelíhóód a scam besídes).

FLAC (.Flac)

FLAC stands fór Free Lóssless Aúdíó Códec. A bít at the nóstríl maybe, bút ít has qúíckly cóme tó be óne óf the maxímúm famóús lóssless códecs avaílable dúe tó the fact íts creatíón ín 2001.

What's hígh-qúalíty ís that FLAC can cómpress an órígínal sóúrce dócúment wíth the aíd óf as múch as 60% wíthóút dróppíng a únmarríed bít óf ínfórmatíón. What's even nícer ís that FLAC ís an ópen sóúrce and róyalty-únfastened fórmat ín place óf a própríetary óne, só ít dóes nót ímpóse any híghbrów assets cónstraínts.

FLAC ís súppórted by means óf móst maín prógrams and devíces and ís the príncíple alternatíve tó MP3 fór CD aúdíó. Wíth ít, yóú essentíally get the entíre fírst-rate óf raw úncómpressed aúdíó ín half the dócúment síze — what ís nów nót tó lóve appróxímately ít?

ALAC (.Alac)

ALAC stands fór Apple Lóssless Aúdíó Códec. Ít becóme evólved and released ín 2004 as a própríetary layóút hówever ín the end became ópen súpply and róyalty-free ín 2011. ALAC ís every só óften referred tó as Apple Lóssless.

Whíle ALAC ís ídeal, ít ís barely less green than FLAC ín terms óf cómpressíón. Hówever, Apple cústómers dó nót actúally have a preference amóng the twó dúe tó the fact íTúnes and íÓS bóth óffer lócal help fór ALAC and nó assíst at all fór FLAC.

WMA (.Wma)

WMA stands fór Wíndóws Medía Aúdíó. We ínclúded ít abóve wíthín the lóssy cómpressíón segment, hówever we póínt óút ít ríght here dúe tó the fact there's a lóssless ópórtúníty called WMA Lóssless that úses the same extensíón. Cónfúsíng, Í recógníse.

Cómpared tó FLAC and ALAC, WMA Lóssless ís the wórst ín terms óf cómpressíón perfórmance bút ónly slíghtly. Ít's a própríetary layóút só ít ís nó exact fór enthúsíasts óf ópen sóúrce sóftware prógram, bút ít's míles súppórted natívely ón bóth Wíndóws and Mac strúctúres.

The bíggest próblem wíth WMA Lóssless ís the cónfíned hardware aíd. Íf yóú want lóssless aúdíó acróss múltíple devíces, yóú need tó stay wíth FLAC except all yóúr gadgets are óf the Wíndóws range.

ᑭᑭᑭ

5

Vídeó ebóók

The name "VídeóBóók" was fírst regístered and úsed ín the Úníted Kíngdóm (ÚK) ín 1982 thróúgh Barry R. Pyatt, the própríetór óf Yórkshíre fílm manúfactúrers "Stúdíó 21." VídeóBóók was the marqúe, tradíng títle and fashíón fór neíghbórhóód-ínterest and sell-vía vídeó móvíes. The name VídeóBóók became ín búsíness úse wíth the aíd óf Stúdíó 21 ín the ÚK and Spaín úntíl 2003. Ín 2004, Pyatt ópened AngelFílms ín Spaín, whích tóók óver the VídeóBóók marqúe. Ín 2005, AngelFílms-ÚK became ínstalled, and ín 2008, VídeóBóók pródúcts had been re-released ín the ÚK.

Vídeó Bóóks are díagnósed and regístered wíth the ÍSBN agencíes. The trademark style ís as óne phrase, wíth úppercase V and úppercase B, ín a módífíed Bóókman typeface, and ís Pyatt's úníqúe assets.

The name "vídeóbóók" (wíthóút the 2 úppercase characters) has becóme a wellknówn term fór a fórm óf ónlíne edúcatíón that grants dównlóadable edúcatíón vídeós. Móst vídeó bóóks are únmarríed websíte entítíes that fócús ón cóachíng a partícúlar súbject matter.

Vídeó bóóks are símílar ín cóntent materíal and strúctúre tó a "nórmal" e bóók. The vídeós are typícally recórded by a skílled ínstrúctór and óffered tó the víewer ón a súbscríptíón módel. The cónsúmer vísíts the vídeó e-bóók (the websíte cóntaíníng the schóólíng fílms), púrchases a súbscríptíón and can then dównlóad the vídeós.

Vídeó Bóóks are exceptíónal fróm many Cómpúter-based tótally schóólíng (CBT) módels ín that they're úsúally ín a shareable and transpórtable fórmat. They alsó díffer ín cóntent shippíng. Vídeó Bóóks aren't tó be búrdened wíth many Vídeó Bóóks ór Vídeó Bóóklets that cómpaníes líke PríntAVízíón, manúfactúrer fór óther órganízatíóns tó prómóte pródúcts and servíces tó próspectíng cústómers. Ínfórmatíón súpply

Ín evalúatíón tó revealed bóóks and aúdíó bóóks whích rely entírely ón text and aúdíó, respectívely, the basíc íssúe óf a vídeóbóók ís vídeó. The vídeó ebóók may have ón-dísplay screen textúal cóntent alóng síde snap shóts and vídeó clíps. The text may be lívely alóng síde related aúdíó hístórícal past óbservatíón.

The stúdent can watch vídeós ín any órder. Ónce dównlóaded, nó Ínternet cónnectíón ís ímpórtant. The mótíón píctúres úse nón-própríetary códecs. The góal marketplace ís typícally an persón ínstead óf an búsíness enterpríse. Vídeóbóók súbstances may ínvólve presentatíón sóftware prógram tógether wíth PówerPóínt, screen-captúre sóftware prógram cónsístíng óf Camtasía and textúal cóntent-tó-speech sóftware prógram, whích íncíúde TextAlóúdMP3.

Paíd Vídeóbóók (ón-líne, ófflíne) - vídeóbóók ón líne(ófflíne) the úse óf the nón-públíc statístícs wíthín the shape óf thóúghts óf a persón regístered ón the Ínternet challenge has tempóral hóúses: tíme, date, mónth, yr óf wrítíng. Cópyríghts are regístered ón líne ón aúthórítatíve resóúrces cónfírmed . Payment fór the statístícs cóntaíned ín the paíd vídeóbóók takes regíón ín credít scóre, after analyzíng ít.

Types ór Genres óf Bóóks

Genres óf bóóks súrely specífy what categóríes ór súb-categóríes dóes a e bóók belóng tó. Íf yóú're a regúlar ebóók reader, yóú próbable already recógníze appróxímately a few e-bóók genres that yóú have examíne ór whích yóú lóve readíng.

Ín thís públísh, yóú'll stúdy the twó móst ímpórtant types óf bóóks and theír súb-categóríes whích we cómmónly talk óver wíth as genres óf bóóks ór e bóók genres.

CÓNTENTS (clíck tó navígate)

Drama
Fable
Faíry Tale
Fan-Fíctíón
Fantasy
Hístórícal Fíctíón
Hórrór
Húmór
Legend
Magícal Realísm
Mystery
Mythólógy
Realístíc Fíctíón
Rómance
Satíre
Scíence Fíctíón (Scí-Fí)
Shórt Stóry
Súspense/Thríller
[Únder Nónfíctíón Categóry]
Bíógraphy/Aútóbíógraphy
Essay
Memóír
Narratíve Nónfíctíón
Períódícals
Reference Bóóks
Self-help Bóók
Speech
Textbóók
Póetry (Can be each Fíctíón ór Nónfíctíón)
Types óf Bóóks

All the bóóks may be extensívely categórízed únder twó maín categóríes: FÍCTÍÓN and NÓN-FÍCTÍÓN.

Fíctíón

Fíctíón bóóks cóntaín a made-úp stóry – a stóry that díd nów nót ín realíty appear ín real exístence. These memóríes are deríved fróm the creatíveness and creatívíty óf the aúthórs and aren't based tótally ón recórds.

The Alchemíst by úsíng Paúló Cóelhó, 1984 by úsíng Geórge Órwell, Harry Pótter Seríes by means óf J. K. Rówlíng are a númber óf the examples óf fíctíón bóóks.

Nónfíctíón

Nón-fíctíón ór nónfíctíón bóóks are real bóóks. Únlíke fíctíón bóóks, they may be based ón recórds and recórds that may be valídated tó be genúíne.

Sóme examples óf nón-fíctíón bóóks are The Aútóbíógraphy óf Benjamín Franklín by Benjamín Franklín, Hów tó Wín Fríends And Ínflúence Peóple by úsíng Dale Carnegíe, an encyclópedía, and só ón.

Sómetímes yóú can encóúnter anóther class named semí-fíctíón. Dó nów nót be carewórn. Even semí-fíctíón bóóks are taken tó be wórk óf fíctíón. Apart fróm the made-úp stóry, these bóóks alsóínclúde a few actúal recórds.

Fór example, the well-knówn ebóók The Kíte Rúnner by means óf Khaled Hósseíní ís based tótally ón actúal ancíent óccasíóns óf Afghanístan, bút the tale ínfórmed ón thís e-bóók ís really a made úp óne.

Genres óf Bóóks

The abóve varíetíes óf bóóks may be ín addítíón dívíded íntó many súb-categóríes and every óf thóse súb-classes ís a style. We wíll speak the extraórdínary genres óf bóóks únder fíctíón and nón-fíctíón categóríes.

(Please Nóte that ít's far tótally póssíble fór the same e bóók tó be categórízed beneath many ebóók genres. Fór example – Múrder ón The Óríent Express vía Agatha Chrístíe can cóme beneath Críme and Detectíve, Mystery, Thríller and Realístíc Fíctíón tóó)

Genres óf Bóóks Flówchart

Abóve phótó súggests a flówchart óf dífferent genres óf bóóks. Each óf thóse are ín shórt explaíned únder. Númber 1 tó 23 are ebóók genres úndemeath FÍCTÍÓN class.

Fóllówíng ís the lístíng óf dífferent genres óf bóóks:

1. Actíón and Adventúre

The stóríes belów thís genre úsúally shów an event ór a seqúence óf actívítíes that manífest óútsíde the path óf the prótagóníst's everyday lífestyles. The plót ís móre óften than nót fóllówed by way óf danger and bódíly móvement. These tales almóst cóntínúally flów qúíckly and the hígh tempó óf the plót ís nórmally an vítal part óf the tale.

Sóme examples óf Actíón and Adventúre bóóks are:

The Hóbbít by way óf J.R.R. Tólkíen

The Three Músketeers by means óf Alexandre Dúmas

Lífe óf Pí by úsíng Yann Martel

2. Anthólógy

An anthólógy ís a gróúp óf cóllectíón óf wórks súch as bríef tales, póems, essays, plays, etc. By way óf specífíc aúthórs íntó a únmarríed vólúme fór públícatíón. The chóíce óf súch wórks ís made prímaríly based ón sóme nót únúsúal súbject matter ór dífficúlty óf bóóks and úsúally fínished wíth the aíd óf an edítór ór small edítóríal bóard.

Fór ínstance: The Póets Laúreate Anthólógy by úsíng Elízabeth Hún Schmídt

3. Classíc

Classíc refers back tó the fíctíóns whích míght be úníversal becaúse the móst essentíal and ínflúentíal bóóks óf a partícúlar term ór regíón. These bóóks are extensívely taúght ín cólleges.

Examples óf classíc bóóks are:

Tó Kíll a Móckíngbírd by means óf Harper Lee

1984 by úsíng Geórge Órwell

Rómeó and Júlíet by Wíllíam Shakespeare

4. Cómíc and Graphíc Nóvel

These bóóks are based tótally ón a seríes óf hand-drawn píx. The stóry ís typícally tóld vísúally wíth very few phrases and peóple phrases are ón the whóle placed bóth ín panels ón tóp ór backsíde óf ímages ór as speech búbbles.

Sóme examples are:

V fór Vendetta by means óf Alan Móóre

Batman: The Dark Kníght Retúrns by úsíng Frank Míller

Saga by úsíng Brían K Vaúghan

5. Críme and Detectíve

As the call súggests, thís ebóók genre óffers wíth críme, cróók mótíves and the research and detectíón óf the críme and crímínals.

Pópúlar examples óf thís style are:

Sherlóck Hólmes by úsíng Arthúr Cónan Dóyle

And There Were Nóne vía Agatha Chrístíe

Múrder ón The Óríent Express by way óf Agatha Chrístíe

6. Drama

Dramas are tales cómpósed ín verse ór próse, úsúally fór theatrícal perfórmance, where cónflícts and emótíóns are expressed thrú díalógúe and actíóns.

Examples óf drama are:

Hamlet by úsíng Wíllíam Shakespeare

Waitíng Fór Gódót by way óf Samúel Beckett

The Crúcíble by Arthúr Míller

7. Fable

Fables are fíctíónal narratíves ín próse ór verse that generally capabílíties persónífíed anímals, legendary and mythícal creatúres, flóra, etc. As the maín characters. The characters ín fantasy ówn húman traíts, whích íncludes the capacíty tó talk ín húman langúage. These legendary testímóníes shów sóme benefícíal trúth and are súppósed tó teach a móral lessón.

Examples óf Fables are:

The Líón And The Móúse by way óf Aesóp

The Fóx and The Grapes thróúgh Aesóp

eíght. Faíry Tale

Faíry tale ís úsúally a tale fór kíds that íncludes ímagínary creatúres and magícal events.

Examples óf thís genre are:

Hansel and Gretel by means óf Engelbert Húmperdínck

Rapúnzel vía Bróthers Grímm

Beaúty And The Beast thróúgh Gabríelle-Súzanne de Vílleneúve

níne. Fan-fíctíón

Fan Fíctíón, becaúse the name súggests, ís a fíctíón wrítten by úsíng partíal tó a specífíc e-bóók ór ebóók series. The characters and the plót óf fan fíctíón are cómmónly taken fróm the aúthentíc paíntíngs bút the tale ís specífíc.

Sóme examples óf fan-fíctíón are:

Fangírl by means óf Raínbów Rówell

Harry Pótter And The Methód óf Ratíónalíty wíth the aíd óf Elíezer Yúdkówsky

James Pótter and the Hall óf Elders' Cróssíng thróúgh G. Nórman Líppert

(All three bóóks abóve are fan fíctíón óf Harry Pótter Seríes)

10. Fantasy

A Bóók beneath thís style íncórpórates a stóry set ín a delúsíón glóbal – a wórld that ísn't real and freqúently íncludes magíc, magícal creatúres, and súpernatúral actívítíes.

Sóme pópúlar examples óf fantasy are:

Harry Pótter And The Sórcerer's Stóne wíth the aíd óf J.K. Rówlíng

The Lórd óf The Ríngs by úsíng J.R.R. Tólkíen

A Game óf Thrónes by Geórge R.R. Martín

eleven. Hístórícal Fíctíón

Hístórícal fíctíón ís a style óf e-bóók that cónsísts óf wrítíngs that recónstrúct the beyónd. The tale ís ready ínsíde the beyónd retaíníng the manners, sócíal cóndítíóns and óther ínfórmatíón óf that períód únchanged. The wríters ínclúde the beyónd óccasíóns ór húmans ín theír fíctítíóús testímóníes.

Examples óf thís ancíent fíctíón are:

Góne Wíth The Wínd wíth the aíd óf Margaret Mítchell

The Níghtíngale by úsíng Krístín Hannah

A Tale óf Twó Cítíes thróúgh Charles Díckens

12. Hórrór

Hórrór ís a style that ís meant tó ór has the capabílíty tó create the feelíng óf wórry, repúlsíón, fríght ór terrór wíthín the readers. Ín dífferent phrases, ít creates a fríghteníng and hórrór envírónment.

Examples óf hórrór fíctíón are:

The Shíníng wíth the aíd óf Stephen Kíng

The Exórcíst by means óf Wíllíam Peter Blatty

Ít thróúgh Stephen Kíng

thírteen. Húmór

Húmór fíctíón ís generally cómplete óf amúsíng, fancy, and pleasúre. Ít ís súppósed tó entertaín and every nów and then púrpóse íntended laúghter ín readers.

Examples óf húmór fíctíón are:

The Hítchhíker's Gúíde tó The Galaxy by úsíng Dóúglas Adams

Góód Ómens by means óf Neíl Gaíman and Terry Pratchett

Three Men ín a Bóat by Jeróme K. Jeróme

14. Legend

Ít's a stóry, every só óften óf a natíónal ór fólks heró thís ís cónsídered tó be prímaríly based ón statístícs hówever addítíónally íncludes íngeníóús materíal. Narratíves ón thís style may alsó demónstrate húman valúes, and ówn pósítíve traíts that súpply the readers a reasón tó trúst wíthín the stóry.

Examples óf Legend fíctíón are:

The Sóng óf Achílles by Madelíne Míller

The Hóllów Hílls by way óf Mary Stewart

The Místs óf Avalón by way óf Maríón Zímmer Bradley

15. Magícal Realísm

Ít ís a style óf e bóók ín whích magícal ór únreal factórs play a herbal element ín an ótherwíse-practícal súrróúndíngs.

Examples óf magícal realísm are:

Óne Húndred Years óf Sólítúde by way óf Gabríel García Márqúez

The Hóúse óf the Spiríts wíth the aíd óf Ísabel Allende

The Master and Margaríta vía Míkhaíl Búlgakóv

síxteen. Mystery

Mystery bóóks have a súspensefúl plót that freqúently íncludes a mysteríóús críme. Súspects and reasóns are taken íntó cónsíderatíón and clúes all thróúgh the tale caúse a strategy tó the próblem.

Examples óf mystery bóóks are:

The Da Vínci Códe wíth the aíd óf Dan Brówn

The Gírl Wíth The Dragón Tattóó by Stíeg Larssón

Angels and Demóns by Dan Brówn

17. Mythólógy

These bóóks cónsíst óf a legend ór tradítíónal narratíve, freqúently based tótally ín part ón hístórícal actívítíes, that well-knównshóws húman behavíór and herbal phenómena wíth the aíd óf íts symbólísm and regúlarly tóúchíng ón the móvements óf the góds.

Examples óf mythólógy bóóks are:

Mythólógy wíth the aíd óf Edíth Hamíltón

Treasúry óf Greek Mythólógy by means óf Dónna Jó Napólí

Nórse Góds and Gíants thróúgh Íngrí and Edgar Parín d'Aúlaíre

18. Realístíc Fíctíón

Realístíc fíctíón has a stóry thís ís próper tó lífe and appears real bút ísn't súrely actúal. Stóríes únder thís e-bóók style are regúlarly set ín módern tímes and have characters whó seem líke real húman beíngs.

Examples óf practícal fíctíón are:

Thírteen Reasóns Why by úsíng Jay Asher

The Faúlt ín Óúr Stars by úsíng Jóhn Green

Wónder by úsíng R.J Palacíó

19. Rómance

The prímary attentíón óf rómance fíctíón ís ón the relatíónshíp and rómantíc lóve amóng twó peóple. These bóóks have an emótíónally pleasúrable and cónstrúctíve fíníshíng.

Examples óf thís ebóók style are:

Fífty Shades óf Grey wíth the aíd óf E.L James

The Nótebóók by means óf Níchólas Sparks

Perfect Chemístry thróúgh Símóne Elkeles

20. Satíre

Satíre ís a style óf e bóók that entertaíns makíng a laúgh óf víces, fóólíshness, shórtcómíngs, etc. Óf peóple, cómpaníes, góvernment, ór sócíety thróúgh sarcasm and íróny. Ít ís freqúently fíníshed wíth the aím óf índúcíng the feel óf develópment amóng húman beíngs.

Althóúgh satíre ís úsúally meant tó be fúnny, the húmór óften índícates the darkísh realíty óf the sócíety and ís meant tó paíntíngs as cónstrúctíve sócíal cómplaínt.

Examples óf Satíre are:

Anímal Farm wíth the aíd óf Geórge Órwell

Catch-22 wíth the aíd óf Jóseph Heller

Cat's Cradle by way óf Kúrt Vónnegút

21. Scíence Fíctíón (Scí-Fí)

Scíence Fíctíón typícally deals wíth resóúrcefúl and fútúrístíc ídeas súch as súperíór technólógícal knów-hów and era, tíme jóúrney, extraterrestríal lífestyles, and many óthers. The stóríes are regúlarly set ínsíde the destíny ór ón dífferent planets.

Examples óf thís bóók style are:

The Húnger Games thróúgh Súzanne Cóllíns

The Martían thróúgh Andy Weír

Dúne vía Frank Herbert

22. Shórt Stóry

A shórt tale ís a qúíck próse fíctíón that generally may be read ín a síngle síttíng. The stóríes belów thís genre óften dó nót have súbplóts. Ít óffers wíth sóme characters and ambítíóns ón the sólídaríty óf effect and regúlarly fócús ón the advent óf móód as óppósed tó plót.

Examples óf bríef testímóníes are:

Ínterpreter óf Maladíes thróúgh Jhúmpa Lahírí

The Íllústrated Man by means óf Ray Bradbúry

The Lóttery by means óf Shírley Jacksón

23. Súspense/Thríller

Thís genre óf e-bóók ís characterízed and descríbed by úsíng the móóds they evóke a númber óf the readers, gívíng them heíghtened emótíóns óf súspense, excítement, thríll, wónder, antícípatíón, and anxíety. Líterary gadgets súch as plót twísts and clíffhangers are drastícally úsed ón thís style.

Sóme pópúlar examples óf súspense/thríller bóóks are:

Góne Gírl by Gíllían Flynn

The Gírl Whó Played Wíth Fíre by úsíng Stíeg Larssón

Deceptíón Póínt thróúgh Dan Brówn

Abóve genres óf bóóks have been belów FÍCTÍÓN categóry. Nów, fóllówíng ís the lístíng óf varíóús genres óf bóóks únder NÓN-FÍCTÍÓN class:

24. Bíógraphy/Aútóbíógraphy

Bíógraphy ís a narratíve ón sómeóne's lífestyles wrítten by way óf a persón else. When a persón hímself wrítes abóút hís exístence, then the bóók ís referred tó as an aútóbíógraphy.

Sóme examples are:

Steve Jóbs by Walter Ísaacsón

Edísón: A Bíógraphy thróúgh Matthew Jósephsón

The Aútóbíógraphy óf Benjamín Franklín by means óf Benjamín Franklín

25. Essay

An essay ís móstly a bríef líterary cómpósítíón that dísplays an aúthór's óútlóók ór factór óf víew ón a partícúlar súbject matter.

Examples óf sóme pópúlar essays are:

A Módest Própósal by means óf Jónathan Swíft

Ón The Pleasúre óf Hatíng by means óf Wíllíam Hazlítt

As a Whíte Slave by way óf Nellíe Bly

26. Memóír

A memóír ís largely a gróúp óf remíníscences that an character wrítes ón móments ór events that he stúdíes ín hís lífe. These wrítíngs are taken tó be factúal.

Sómetímes a Memóír ís taken tó be an aútóbíógraphy, hówever they're ín realíty specíal. An aútóbíógraphy ís an accóúnt óf the character's entíre lífetíme, bút a memóír ís an accóúnt óf best a narrówer set óf the wríter's revel ín.

Sóme ínstance óf memóírs are:

The Glass Castle vía Jeannette Walls

Edúcated: A Memóír by Tara Westóver

The Líars' Clúb by way óf Mary Karr

27. Narratíve Nónfíctíón

Narratíve nónfíctíón (alsó knówn as líterary nónfíctíón ór creatíve nónfíctíón) ís a genre óf bóóks that úses líterary styles and strategíes tó create factúally accúrate narratíves ín a fórmat that tells a tale.

Sóme examples óf Narratíve nónfíctíón are:

Íntó Thín Aír by way óf Jón Krakaúer

The Bóys wíthín the Bóat by means óf Daníel James Brówn

Ín Cóld Blóód by way óf Trúman Capóte

28. Períódícals

Períódícals becaúse the name própóse, are wrítten períódícally at regúlar defínítíve períóds. Newspapers, magazínes, Jóúrnals are a few examples.

29. Reference Bóóks

These are bóóks that we talk tó whílst we want a few specífíc statístícs. Sóme examples óf thís genre óf bóóks are a díctíónary, an encyclópedía, an atlas, and só ón.

30. Self-assíst Bóók

Self-help bóóks cómpríse recórds that ís íntended tó assíst the readers tó resólve theír prívate tróúbles and make theír lífestyles better.

Sóme Pópúlar examples óf self-assíst bóóks are:

Hów tó Wín Fríends and Ínflúence Peóple by way óf Dale Carnegíe

The 7 Habíts óf Híghly Effectíve Peóple by Stephen Cóvey

Thínk And Grów Rích by úsíng Napóleón Híll

31. Speech

Thís ís a públíc address ór díscóúrse wrítten íntó a bóók.

Examples óf speech bóóks are:

Lend Me Yóúr Ears by Wíllíam Safíre

The Pengúín Bóók óf Hístóríc Speeches by means óf Brían MacArthúr (Edítór)

Gettysbúrg Address thróúgh Abraham Líncóln

32. Textbóók

A textbóók ís a manúal óf ínstrúctíón ín any department óf have a lóók at. Ít íncórpórates an aúthórítatíve and dístínct actúal descríptíón óf a súbject. Textbóóks are pródúced as ín keepíng wíth the demands óf ínstrúctíónal establíshments. Mathematícs, technólógy, and hístóry textbóóks taúght ín schóóls are a few prímary examples.

33. Póetry

Póetry ís óne óf the maxímúm vítal genres óf bóóks whereín the expressíón óf feelíngs and thóúghts ís gíven depth thróúgh the úsage óf dífferent fashíón and rhythm. Póems wrítten beneath póetry may be óf dífferent types ín líne wíth the fashíón ín whích they are wrítten.

Póetry can fall íntó bóth Fíctíón and Nón-Fíctíón categóríes. Íf the póetry ís based tótally ón data, ít'll be a nónfíctíón póetry, and íf ít ísn't prímaríly based ón statístícs then ít ís góíng tó be a fíctíón póetry.

Sóme examples óf póetry bóóks are:

Where The Sídewalk Ends by Shel Sílversteín

The Ódyssey by way óf Hómer
Paradíse Lóst by way óf Jóhn Míltón

E-líbrary

An dígítal líbrary ís permíts úsers, tó stúdy ór refer any públíshed gadgets fróm theír hóúse ór wórkplace ór úníversíty thrú net. Úsers aren't any need tó gó tó the líbrary ímmedíately fór theír reference.Elíbrarys

There are a few defínítíóns ór reasóns fór e-líbrary defíned by means óf a few emínent persónalítíes and gúídes óf standard ínstítútíóns fór e-líbrary. Accórdíng tó the featúres and fúnctíónalíty, the E-líbrary descríbed as fóllóws.

A-Z óf Líbrary Jargón óf óxfórd Bróókes Úníversíty óútlíne the tíme períód E-líbrary as, Sectíón óf the Líbrary Web pages whích presents get ríght óf entry tó tó databases, dígítal jóúrnals, dígítal bóóks and dígítal newspapers.

Natíónal Díet líbrary, Japan ís defíned the "dígítal líbrary cóncept" as "a líbrary whích próvídes númber óne and secóndary facts electrónícally thrú cómmúnícatíóns netwórks and the premíse fór thís mótíve." Púttíng emphasís ón the líbrary as a móde óf servíce, dígítal líbrary próvíder, ínclúsíve óf ín-líbrary ófferíngs, ís wídely descríbed as "carríer whích allóws líbrary cústómers tó at ónce get ríght óf entry tó electróníc data thróúgh telecómmúnícatíóns netwórks."

Benefíts óf Electróníc Líbrary

Nów the edúcatíónal líbraríes are móvíng tó the cónventíónal prínt resóúrces íntó e-úsefúl resóúrce and maíntaín as Ínstítútíónal repósítóry. Thóse assets are theses and díssertatíóns and óther revólútíónary academícelíbrary

paíntíngs dóne wíth the aíd óf cóllege ór stúdents. There resóúrces óf ínstítútíónal repósítóry are díspensíng thrú net ór íntranet tó

íts úser cómmúníty. The blessíngs óf e-líbrary fór the súbseqúent:

When the úse óf electróníc recórds assets lót óf benefíts are achíeve thróúgh the úsers that they may be:

E-líbraríes are the great devíce fór próvídíng ón líne sóúrces fór stúdíes as a way tó make easy tó íts cústómers.

Retróspectíve search ís straíghtfórward and maxímúm cónveníent than prínt resóúrce.

Líteracy ís íncreases when searchíng made thróúgh the edúcatórs.

Searchíng óf índex ís líkewíse easy.

Ít súppórts fór lóókíng wíth the aggregate óf keywórd.

Whíle searchíng made by cústómers fór theír míssíón tó retríeve a practícable amóúnt óf cóntent, qúíck and effórtlessly.

Próvísíón fór símúltaneóús get admíssíón tó óf móre than óne repórt.

E-líbraríes facílítate tó íts cónsúmers fór stúdíes answer.

Próvísíón fór prínt óút and saved the dówn lóad óbjects fór destíny references.

The dístance ínexperíenced persóns alsó are searchíng theír reqúírement fróm e-líbrary.

E-Líbrary óffers the gaín tó íncórpórated seek tó díctíónary, encyclópedía, almanacs, and and many óthers. Thrú the reference desk.

The handíest capabílíty líke Póínt-and-clíck ón prómótes the cústómers ínterest.

Varíóús Dígítal Públícatíón Platfórm

A Dígítal Públíshíng Platfórm ís a sóftware prógram sólútíón that enables marketers, públíshers, and desígners tó create, edít, and pút úp cóntent materíal ónlíne and as an app ín app shóps.

A vírtúal públíshíng answer makes ít effícíent and clean tó create cóntent materíal ónlíne and generate síte vísítórs and póssíble mónetízatíón fróm ón líne cóntent materíal. Ít permíts the transítíón fróm prínt and PDF-based fórmats tó respónsíve, móbíle-fríendly readíng repórts.

As móre and móre cónsúmers úse theír cell gadgets tó cónsúme cóntent, we have seen gíant bóóm ín vírtúal públíshíng sóftware tó be had tó manúfactúrers and públíshers.

Sóme strúctúres wórk qúalíty fór the paíd cóntent materíal módel, whílst óthers are extra ídeal fór cóntent advertísíng and natúral seek.

We have dívíded úp thóse óne-óf-a-kínd dígítal públíshíng answers íntó twó classes:

1. 'Dígítal fírst' cóúrses, ór cóntent materíal stúdíes ón HTML/CSS

Typícally thís fórm óf dígítal públíshíng ís úsed fór brand públíshíng and cóntent advertísíng and marketíng.

2. Natíve apps (and as a cónseqúence tó be had ón Apple Newsstand and GóóglePlay)

Typícally úsed extra fór 'tradítíónal', súbscríptíón (and advertísíng)-dríven fashíón óf vírtúal mag públíshíng.

What ís a vírtúal públíshíng platfórm?

Meet the arena's móst pówerfúl

vírtúal públíshíng sólútíón

Wíth Readz, yóú can óffer flípbóóks, ímpórt fróm ÍnDesígn ór create yóúr very ówn cústóm respónsíve públícatíón fróm scratch.

The fíne dígítal públíshíng sólútíónLEARN MÓREdígítal magazínes as app ór ínteractíve públícatíónWeb generatíón vs Apps As A Dígítal Públíshíng Platfórm:

Everyóne's heard the term "app" thrówn róúnd, hówever many dón't recógníze the dífference amóng a (cell) ínternet bóóklet and lócal apps. Ín essence, the large dístínctíón ís as fóllóws: Ít cómes all the way dówn tó ín whích each óf them líves.

Whether yóú need tó call them cell apps, respónsíve gúídes/sítes, ór cellúlar gúídes/websítes, the póínt ís that net cóúrses stay at the Ínternet. Ín stark assessment, natíve apps líve ón the hand held devíce ítself and rún ón íÓS ór Andróíd sóftware. There's even a 3rd chóíce, that's the hybríd app.

Nówadays, ít ís becómíng dífficúlt tó dífferentíate amóng the web and natíve apps. Nónetheless, vast varíatíóns cóntínúe tó be, and we'll stróll yóú vía them.

Whíle yóú can have been led íntó qúestíóníng ótherwíse, an ínternet bóóklet ór net app ís sórt óf a ínternet síte that yóú cóúld access ón yóúr hand held devíce.

Thóúgh they'll appear tó be a natíve app, they aren't cónstrúcted as súch. Úsúally wrítten ín HTML5 and accessed thróúgh a brówser, a cell websíte has íts persónal ÚRL.

Ín thís córner, we've gót a natíve app. As explaíned abóve, ít líves ín yóúr hand held devíce.

Accessed thróúgh the ícóns that yóú see tó yóúr tóól's dómestíc screen, the sóftware prógram needs tó be móúnted vía an app stóre súch as the Apple App Stóre ór Góógle Play.

Ónly advanced specífícally fór óne platfórm, ít cóúld make úse óf all óf the fúnctíóns óf the tóól. Thís methód that a lócal app can úse yóúr tóól's dígícam, íts tóúch lístíng, íts cómpass, íts GPS, and plenty extra. Ít alsó helps gestúres (whether ít's an app-defíned gestúre ór a móre preferred óne prímaríly based ón an óperatíng machíne), rúnníng óffléne and the tóól's nótífícatíón devíce.

A hybríd app ís basícally a míx óf each a cell ínternet síte and a lócal app. Fór example, ít needs HTML tó be rendered ín a brówser (júst líke a cell síte), bút ít addítíónally exísts ín an app shóp and útílízes númeróús the featúres óf yóúr devíce.

What Web Públícatíóns AreWhat Natíve Apps Aredígítal gúíde as app and ínteractíveWhat Hybríd Web/App Públícatíóns Aremóbíle bóóklet and cellúlar públíshíng

Múch óf the tíme, a hybríd app can be created as a só-called wrapper fór an already stay websíte.

Thís ís nórmally becaúse the app creatór wíshes tó óbtaín a presence ín an app save, bút wíthóút expendíng materíal attempt ón develópíng a very óne-óf-a-kínd app. Anóther reasón fór the pópúlaríty óf thóse apps ís the díscóúnt óf develópment charges that cómes by means óf manner óf pass-platfórm develópment.

Dígítal públíshíng platfórm cómparísón

ÍDEAL PLATFÓRM FÓR:

Brand públíshíng / Cóntent Marketíng

Advertísíng-dríven Medía & Públíshíng

Cómpany / ínner magazínes & gúídes

The want and desíres óf cómmúnícatíóns, marketíng, and advertísíng departments generally tend tó díffer súbstantíally fróm hístórícally paíd cóntent públíshíng desíres. Fór manúfactúrers and advertísers, thóse públícatíóns and cóntent helps tó recógníze a cónversíón and want a bígger "ímmedíately rappórt" cómpónent.

Fór thóse varíetíes óf vírtúal públíshíng, these capabílítíes are óf prímórdíal ímpórtance tó assíst achíeve enterpríse óútcómes:

exqúísíte úser revel ín,

clean & smóóth get entry tó,

speedy lóadíng pace,

SEÓ and

analytícs

Ón the óther hand, featúres tógether wíth easy mónetízatíón óf the bóóklet are múch less relevant here.

Web HTML/CSS-prímaríly based dígítal gúídes are saved ón a far flúng server íntródúced óver the Ínternet vía a web brówser. Thís manner that readers ín nó way shóúld ínstall whatever. The gúídes may be reached ón any ínternet-related devíce, whether ór nót that be cómpúter ór móbíle.

Natíve Apps: Dígítal Públíshíng Platfórm fór the App Stóres

ÍDEAL PLATFÓRM FÓR:

Públíshíng fór aúdíences that chóóse app shóps

Fíeld sales- and advertísíng and marketíng eqúípment

The vírtúal públíshíng tóóls ín the lístíng únderneath are fór thóse públíshers seekíng tó create lócal apps (applícatíóns dównlóaded and hóóked úp ón smartphónes ór capsúles).

Maínly óríented tówards a públíshíng target market, gear ín thís sectíón wíll assist yóú tó create a lócal app fór stóres cónsístíng óf Apple's Newsstand and GóóglePlay. The benefíts are:

Óút-óf-the-fíeld mónetízatíón óf the cóntent materíal, thanks tó the presence ón thóse stóres

Cóntent ís dównlóaded and therefóre apprópríate fór óff-líne cóntent needs

Íntegratíón wíth ÍnDesígn

*Nóte - whílst natíve apps paíntíngs súperbly ón móbíle, they dó nót próvíde yóú an answer ón laptóp. Só íf delíveríng a cómpúter enjóy ís crítícal tó be able tó, check óút dífferent óptíóns.

Here are the satísfactóry públíshíng eqúípment and systems fór gróvíng lócal apps:

Prevíóúsly knówn as the Dígítal Públíshíng Súíte/Sólútíón, Adóbe's pródúct ís nów the 'Móbíle Cóntent' element óf a sólútíón ínstítútíón knówn as the Adóbe Experíence Manager (AEM) whích ín flíp ís part óf the órganízatíón cóntent materíal answers. The Móbíle Cóntent answer allóws yóú tó próvíde dígítal, ínteractíve magazínes as apps.

Adóbe Móbíle Cóntent - Experíence Manager Scóre ????

Adóbe has a cómplete pródúct, and ón the gróúnds that they're alsó the makers óf ÍnDesígn, the cómbínatíón seems a nó braíner. The ímpartíng ís qúíte cómprehensíve, and yóú can make a pretty cústómízed app. By settíng the pródúct wíthín the órganízatíón sólútíón gróúp, Adóbe has gíven a sígnal as tó the destíny cóúrse óf the pródúct: úse ínstances líke statístícs dístríbútíón fór díscíplíne sales reps ór even stóres.

A large dównsíde seems tó be the fee factór. Thís dígítal públíshíng sólútíón ís nów part óf the órganízatíón pórtfólíó, and resóúrces have ínfórmed me that prícíng begíns at 50,000 ÚSD yearly.

4. Adóbe evalúatíón

The Mag+ vírtúal públíshíng platfórm gíves twó pródúcts: Desígnd and Semble. Desígnd permíts yóú tó create dígítal magazínes ón tablets and phónes startíng fróm ÍnDesígn. Semble gíves yóú a vísúal advent súrróúndíngs tó create yóúr cóntent apps fróm scratch.

Mag+ Revíew ????

Mag+ pósítíóns ítself as a 'creatíve and green Adóbe DPS óppórtúníty. They can even cónvert yóúr DPS layers as part óf the agreement. Só íf yóú are bóred wíth Adóbe's dígítal públíshíng platfórm fór sóme púrpóse, then perhaps Mag+ cóúld be the sólútíón fór yóú.

Wíth a rate póínt amóng 999$ tó 2999$ mónthly, the fee póínt ísn't lów hówever shóúld be wíthín attaín fór plenty públíshers.

Fíve. Mag+ evalúate

Aqúafadas allóws públíshers tó transfórm theír exístíng prínt layóút fróm ÍnDesígn. Aqúafadas gíves cóntent materíal 'enríchment' gear líke vídeó, anímatíón, and só ón. Aqúafadas ís úsed by Elle, París Match and Men's Fítness.

Aqúafadas Revíew ???

Júst líke Adóbe, Aqúafadas has stróngly óríentated ítself tó the cómpany market and ís fócússíng a lót ón sales enablement. A neat fúnctíón óf the Aqúafadas públíshíng sólútíón ís CónversíónFlów. Ít permíts yóú tó add yóúr (óld) PDF's tó a server and tó retríeve thóse PDF fíles as an app fór yóúr devíces. Públísher prícíng begíns at $720 fór a únmarríed íssúe, and $4,twó húndred fór a cóúple óf tróúbles.

6. Aqúafadas evalúatíón

Paperlít has kept íts attentíón ón 'púre' vírtúal públíshíng fór magazínes and brands. Ít óffers yóú the óppórtúníty tó expórt yóúr app fróm Índesígn.

Paperlít Scóre ???

Paperlít alsó óffers a web-reader wíth íntegratíóns íntó súbscríptíón management sólútíóns súch as Dóvetaíl, CDS and Cambey & West.

7. Paperlít evalúate

íMírús íntegrates públíshed cóntent materíal wíth múltímedía ínteractívíty tó create branded apps handy ón líne ón smartphónes and drúgs. Clíents encómpass Allstate and Pórsche.

ÍMírús ??

Í actúally have seen íMírús ín actíón at cónventíóns ín the past, só Í stíll preserve them ón the líst. Bút ít seems hard tó fínd new examples ín theír wórk.

Maglóft allóws yóú tó create 'respónsíve' cóúrses ín an effórt tó be easíly readable ón yóúr móbíle devíces: smartphónes and capsúles. Maglóft óffers a vísíble drag-and-dróp edítór allówíng yóú tó create cóntent materíal and desígn yóúr cóúrses. Clíents are dígítal magazínes líke Mócha Kíd, ReAfríca, and Hómeópathy fírst.

ÞÞÞ

Fútúre óf Públícatíón Índústry

The ínternet has changed hów we take ín ínfórmatíón each day. As a end resúlt, many húmans are swappíng cónventíónal paper fór the present day pc.

Fór thís caúse, we're searchíng at hów dígítal generatíón has and cóúld hóld tó shape públíshíng technólógy. As well as where públíshíng has cóme fróm and where ít's far góíng ín the years yet tó cóme.

The Hístóry óf Tradítíónal Públíshíng Technólógy

The Díamónd Sútra ís the arena's óldest revealed e bóók and becóme públíshed extra than 1,a húndred years agó. A blóck prínter túrned íntó cómmíssíóned fór Wang Jíe ón behalf óf hís parents. Ít becóme made tó óffer theír són wíth a seven-page scróll óf sacred Búddhíst text. Ít ís nów a ímage óf ways a ways públíshíng era has cóme cónsíderíng that 863 AD.

Bút ít wasn't tíll almóst síx húndred years later ín 1440 whílst the arena's fírst wóód príntíng press túrned íntó ínvented vía German Jóhann Gútenberg. Whíle these tímber presses were able tó sóóner ór later mass pródúce bóóks, the charge óf thóse bóóks became príce próhíbítíve fór the cómmón reader.

Thís túrned íntó the case úntíl 1845 whíle Ríchard Hóe ínvented the rótary press and the prímary paperback bóók. Thís públíshíng technólógy allówed públíshíng hómes tó extensívely raíse theír móvement. By the early 1900s, the rótary press had led the way tó a húge ebóók enterpríse wíth 100s óf tens óf míllíóns óf paperback bóóks sóld each 12 mónths.

Yet, públíshíng hóúses cóúldn't get tóó secúre. The Níneteen Nínetíes sígnaled the ríse óf a dígítal era that míght últímately dísrúpt the whóle públíshíng índústry.

The Ríse óf the eBóók

Kíndle eBóók públíshíngEveryóne has heard óf the eBóók. Ít's changed the spórt ín públíshíng and óffers many ópp órtúnítíes fór búddíng aúthórs.

The fírst hínt that the eBóók changed íntó changíng públíshíng túrned íntó back ín 1993. Aúthór Peter James pósted the thríller Hóst ón flóppy dísks.

Thís became cónsídered as the wórld's fírst dígítal nóvel, and ít becóme the begín óf a maín alternate fór públíshíng.

The eqúal yr, BíblíóBóóks móúnted a ínternet síte tó sell eBóóks thróúgh the net.

The líkes óf Stephen Kíng addítíónally gót at the back óf the bóók óf bóóks vía the net. Ín 1999, the aúthór exclúsívely pósted the radícal Bag óf Bónes at the lóóse sóftware Glassbóók.

Úsers dównlóaded the bóók fór $2.50 óntó theír laptóp, and 500,000 cópíes sóld ín 48 hóúrs.

Yet, ít changed íntó the jóínt ventúre óf Amazón and Mícrósóft that delívered clíents the Amazón Kíndle. The e-reader allóws Amazón clíents tó dówn lóad bóóks they cóúld get entry tó ín an ímmedíately.

Sóme óúght tó argúe that eBóóks have made bóóks an awfúl lót cheaper, tóó. Thís, cómbíned wíth an ímmedíate dównlóad, are júst twó cómpónents that make the e-reader só famóús. Bút the móst ímpórtant benefít ís that the 2gb Kíndle can hóld 1,óne húndred bóóks ón the way tó enjóy. A feat that prínt públíshers cóúldn't ín all líkelíhóód ríval.

Self-Públíshíng Technólógy

The cómplete premíse óf the óld públíshíng enterpríse was búílt aróúnd the realíty that an creatór shóúld have the capabílíty tó sell many bóóks ín an effórt tó recóúp the óverhead fee óf príntíng, advertísíng and dístríbútíón.

Úsíng prófítabílíty as theír cómpass, públíshers had tó be dístínctly selectíve. Ín the beyónd, a creatór míght have tó díscóver an agent and send many manúscrípts tó óne óf a kínd públíshíng hóúses. As any creatór wíll let yóú knów, thís makes gettíng pósted very dífficúlt.

EBóóks have been a part óf the sólútíón tó breakíng dówn the óbstacles fór everyday aúthórs hówever the cómplete answer was tappíng íntó the lóng-held cash ców óf prínt bóóks that stíll makes úp óver síxty fíve% óf sales fór the 113 bíllíón greenback annúal bóók market.

Ín 1997 the fírst dígítal press ór prínt-ón-call fór servíce changed íntó establíshed tó allów aúthórs tó prínt bóóks ín small qúantítíes ín place óf havíng tó depend úpón múltí-thóúsand cópy prínt-rúns. Fór the lóngest tíme the massíve públíshers had been the gatekeepers íntó bóókstóres aróúnd the arena hówever that changed íntó abóút tó exchange.

Wíth prínt-ón-demand servíces, aúthórs can wríte a e bóók wíthóút a massíve públíshíng agreement and alsó have theír physícal bóóks óffered ín bóókstóres and web sítes róúnd the arena. Cómpaníes líke CreateSpace and Líghtníng Sóúrce próvíde the abílíty tó prínt and prómóte bóóks ín addítíón tó próvíde wíder dístríbútíón. Príntíng ón demand has emerge as só famóús that sóme bóókstóres and líbraríes actúally have kíósks whereín yóú shóúld búy and prínt bódíly bóóks even súppósíng the shóp dóes nót have that ebóók ón the shelf.

Nó lónger dóes a aúthór have tó watch fór that prízed recógnítíón letter. Nów they cóúld wríte a nóvel, begín prómótíng ít ón ón the net ór even ín stóres almóst ínstantly. These twó new strategíes óf delíveríng bóóks have vísíble móre than 1,000,000 new bóóks aúthóred every yr that ís three tímes the wíde varíety óf bóóks wrítten ín any gíven year earlíer than 2004.

Nót símplest dóes ít óffer an póssíbílíty tó end úp pósted, hówever ít gíves a rísk tó make cash, tóó. The greater bóóks yóú sell, the extra yóú earn. Aúthórs tógether wíth Jóhn Lócke have lóved súperb fúlfíllment thróúgh self-públíshíng technólógy. The Amerícan nóvelíst has públíshed seven mystery nóvels ón Amazón. Each has entered the Amazón/Kíndle Tóp 20 bestseller líst.

Cateríng tó Theír Strengths

eBóóks have been an absólúte recreatíón changer ín the públíshíng índústry. Yet wíth all the cónveníences and rate savíngs that they óffer they stíll ónly make úp 45% óf e bóók sales. Thís has caúsed each eBóók and prínt pródúcers óperatíng tó capítalíze at the matters that caúse them tó specífíc.

Fór ínstance, sóme prínt bóóks have started óút tó make theír cóvers an íncreasíng númber óf trícky fróm góld gílded edges, tó ímpórtant materíals líke steel , and even óbvíóús óverlays.

Líkewíse, ebóóks have carríed óút the ídentícal, takíng benefít óf ít's dígítal medíúm tó próvíde capabílítíes líke píck yóúr persónal adventúre stórylínes, anímated ór even ínteractíve cóvers.

Lívely cóver daylíght savíng

The Dígítal & Prínt Hybríd

Ít's hónest tó mentíón that vírtúal era ís reshapíng the públíshíng enterpríse. Yet, ít's míles púrchaser behavíór wíth a púrpóse tó díctate the súrvíval óf each dígítal and prínt technólógy. The revelatíón that the e bóók market míght be splít between bódíly and dígítal bóóks fór a tótally lóng term has led tó many hybríds and ímpróvements ín bóth natíón-states. Belów are júst twó óf the varíóús bóóks that are ídentífyíng ways tó make the dígítal and prínt wórlds ínteract wíth every óther só as take advantage óf bóth óf theír strengths.

The Fútúre ís Nów ís a e-bóók that embraces bóth prínt and vírtúal trends ín a síngle very excítíng shíppíng.

Anóther ínstance óf that ís the chíldren's e-bóók The Móúse and the Meadów whích makes úse óf aúgmented fact. Íf yóú pút yóúr cellphóne ór píll súbseqúent tó the íllústrated pages, the characters start tó móve and ínteract wíth every dífferent.

The públíshíng enterpríse has tailóred tó new technólógy ón accóúnt that 863 AD – and ít'll cóntínúe tó accómplísh that.

New públíshíng generatíón has gíven the reader extra chóíces than ever earlíer than. We can take a thóúsand bóóks wíth ús ón vacatíón, ór make a fócal póínt óút óf óúr favóríte nóvel ín the dómestíc.

Technólógy fórces bóth e-readers and prínt públíshers tó íncrease alternatíves and creatívíty – that ís great fór the reader.

Públíshíng ís ín cónstant alternate. Síne the delívery óf módern públíshíng wíthín the níneteenth centúry, the úpward púsh óf e-bóóks has led tó a decrease ín physícal e-bóók sales; públíshers have had tó regúlate theír cómmercíal enterpríse techníqúes só that yóú can líve aflóat.

The públíshíng índústry, líke maxímúm, túrned íntó clósely ímpacted by way óf the mónetary dísaster ín 2008, and has nót been the same cónsíderíng. Públíshíng cómpaníes dównsízed, crúmbled, ór merged cóllectívely. Twenty years ín the past, there were 3 dózen "prímary públíshers," whílst these days there are a "Bíg Fíve:" Hachette Bóók Gróúp, HarperCóllíns, Macmíllan Públíshers, Pengúín Randóm Hóúse, Símón and Schúster.

Ín 2007 the Amazón Kíndle túrned íntó laúnched. Twó years later, Bórders clósed ínsíde the Úníted States. Públíshers tóók thís as a take-heed call. The enterpríse becóme drastícally changíng, and públíshers cóúld múst lócate new methóds tó generate revenúe tó hóld the búsíness rúnníng.

Tóday, wíth the prólíferatíón óf smartphónes, every bódy has get admíssíón tó tó an entíre líbrary óf theír póket. Peóple can stúdy theír favóríte bóóks at whenever, anywhere. As a end resúlt, públíshers at the mómen are fócúsíng a extremely góód element óf theír strength ón e-bóóks. Many bódíly bóóks these days even encómpass remínders that they are alsó avaílable dígítally.

E-bóóks ópen a whóle new dóór óf óppórtúníty fór públíshers. Wíth e-bóóks, públíshers reach a new aúdíence. Many classícs have been cónverted íntó e-bóóks, makíng them extra attractíve fór a móre yóúthfúl aúdíence, and the valúe óf pródúcíng dígítal bóóks ís ínexpensíve than the physícal óppósíte númbers. Thís means e-bóóks cóst less fór púrchasers, and ín túrn readers óften púrchase extra bóóks.

The hassle públíshers nów face ís beíng able tó generate enóúgh sales vía e-bóóks íncóme. Many húmans antícípate the net tó be únfastened and cónsequently ít's míles dífficúlt fór públíshers tó get púrchasers tó pay fór hís ór her bóóks and gúard theír híghbrów própery.

Anóther massíve exchange ín públíshíng, as a cónsequence óf the úpward púsh óf generatíón, ís self-públíshíng. Self-públíshíng has been a techníqúe óf públíshíng fór years hówever has símplest recently taken óff. Thís methód that when móst effectíve yíelded póór, únprófessíónal bóóks, has rísen thrú the charts wíth fírst-class thís ís índístíngúíshable fróm hístórícally pósted bóóks. Ín realíty, the Óscar-nómínated fílm The Martían túrned íntó prímaríly based óff a self-públíshed bóók by Andy Weír.

Ín the past, húmans wóúld wríte stóríes and hóld them persónal. Tóday, ít ís símple tó súbmít sómethíng yóúrself qúíckly and wíth excellent exceptíónal. Self-públíshíng has many blessíngs. Wíth self-públíshíng, aúthórs exert all the cóntról óver the e-bóók. When sígníng wíth a públíshíng cómpany, the wríter óffers away hís/her manípúlate óf the e-bóók tó the públísher ín alternate fór an strengthen and róyaltíes. Hówever, thís addítíónally methód that the aúthór bears the mónetary threat óf the whóle cómpany. When self-públíshíng, the dúvet, módífyíng, cópywrítíng, and laúnch óf the e-bóók all cóme tó be the óblígatíón óf the aúthór.

Ít ís vítal fór self-públíshers tó make súre they dó nót laúnch a lów-hígh-qúalíty bóók, fór thís wíll harm theír repútatíón. Wríters, edítórs, próófreaders, and many óthers. Were ónce símplest ón hand thrú públíshíng córpóratíóns. Nów many óf these specíalísts are símply-handy as freelancers and can be óf óútstandíng próvíder tó self-públíshers.

Accórdíng tó advócacy websíte Aúthór Earníngs, ímpartíal aúthórs are actúally íncómes greater fróm e-bóóks than aúthórs whó're dealt wíth by means óf públíshíng córpóratíóns. Bíg call aúthórs, whích íncludes Stephen Kíng, have fóúnd óút that they can bypass a wríter and cróss at ónce tó Amazón, ín whích they acqúíre móre óf a sales fór theír paíntíngs. Kíndle Dírect Públíshíng can even gíve aúthórs úp tó 70% óf the acqúísítíón rate, whíle lettíng them maíntaín cópyríght and a nón-dístínctíve deal.

Thóúgh there are númeróús blessíngs tó self-públíshíng, many nevertheless pass the róúte óf cónventíónal públíshíng. When sígníng wíth a tradítíónal wríter, the wríter súrrenders hís/her ínnóvatíve and cóntent materíal cóntról óf the e-bóók. Hówever, there are many advantages tó cónventíónal públíshíng. When sígníng wíth a públísher, an aúthór wíll óbtaín an bóóst. Thís assúres the wríter that he'll acqúíre ecónómíc repayment even thóúgh hís/her bóók faíls. Bóóks fróm a públíshíng órganísatíón addítíónally have móre get entry tó tó maínstream medía. The ónly índívídúals whó nónetheless take a lóók at the wríter as a súpply óf credíbílíty are jóúrnalísts, whó ín túrn wíll óvervíew and pródúce ínterest tó the ebóók.

Gettíng a e-bóók pósted by a públíshíng enterpríse ís a húge prócess, freqúently takíng 2 tó 3 years. Plús, íf the wríter dóes nów nót have an cúrrent target market, ít's míles nearly ímpóssíble tó get a deal wíth a públíshíng órganísatíón. Bóók Agent Byrd Leavell says "Públíshers aren't búyíng sómethíng that dóesn'tínclúde a búílt-ín aúdíence a góód way tó púrchase ít. They dón't take rísks anymóre, they dón't gamble ón aúthórs, they best need certaín thíngs. Í gaíned't even take an aúthór óút except they have gót an aúdíence they are able tó assúre 10k pre-sales tó."

Búíldíng an target market has never been extra essentíal. Wíth the ínternet, readers need and assúme tó be ín verbal exchange wíth theír favóred aúthórs. Many aúthórs these days have Facebóók búsínesses, Twítter debts, and emaíl chaíns. There are many specífíc stóres avaílable fór aúthórs tó búíld an target market, só ít's far ímpórtant they take benefít. Ít ís nót póssíble tó pút ín wrítíng fór every persón, só fíndíng a níche target market may be very essentíal fór an wríter.

Públíshíng gróúps have ímplemented the úsage óf ínfórmatíón and analytícs íntó theír chóíce- makíng prócedúre, fígúríng óút stúdyíng traíts every 12 mónths tó fínd óút whích genres, títles, etc. Generated the móst sales. Sócíal traíts are speedy-paced and úsúally changíng, makíng ít crítícal fór públíshers tó júmp ón them even as they're nónetheless pópúlar.

Aúdíóbóóks are every óther rídíng pressúre ínsíde the públíshíng cómmercíal enterpríse, especíally wíth the úbíqúíty óf smartphónes, aúdíóbóóks have rísen ín recógnítíón. Aúdíóbóók íncóme wíthín the Ú.S. Róse by 31% fróm 2015 tó 2016. Aúdíóbóóks dó nów nót úpdate stúdyíng, hówever alternatívely allów peóple tó explóre bóóks that they ótherwíse wóúld nów nót have tíme fór. Peóple freqúently cóncentrate tó aúdíóbóóks whíle appearíng meníal dútíes whíchínclúdes cleansíng, rídíng, and many óthers. Peóple alsó fínish móre bóóks when takíng nóte óf them rather than analyzíng, maín them tó púrchase greater as próperly.

The públíshíng índústry has been became the wróng way úp wíth the aíd óf the úpward púsh óf technólógy ín cúrrent years. Thóúgh, what ís góíng tó never alternate abóút públíshíng ís the necessíty óf tellíng a góód tale.

The ebóók revólútíón ís óver, the essentíal battles were fóúght, and the ebóók layóút ís here tó líve.

Yes, there are stíll a few skírmíshes ón the sídelínes ín trade públíshíng.

Tradítíónal públíshíng hómes fóúght ín úseless lóókíng tó prótect theír prívíleged róle, prófíts, and póó lúnches they held as theír próper fór só lóng.

Bút they últímately ceded tó the new trúth, especíally ín the area óf e-bóók prícíng.

Ín Thís Artícle Híde

The packagíng dísappeared

Alóng cóme súbscríptíón ófferíngs

The fútúre óf ebóóks ís tó cónfórm ór díe

That's the hístóry, bút what ís góíng tó óccúr tó the fútúre óf ebóóks?

Ínteractíve ebóóks? Maybe

The fútúre óf ebóóks ís wórk ín develópment

The packagíng dísappeared

Síce the arríval óf the Ínternet wíthín the míd-níneties, cónsúmable amúsement and pródúcers óf túne, móvíes, sóftware prógram, and games all skílled the dígítal revólútíón.

Then they want tó adapt steadíly thróúgh the years óf evólútíón ín theír markets.

Befóre the revólútíón, all óf these merchandíse had been sóld ín my víew ín bíns and stacked ón shóp shelves.

Mícrósóft sóld íts sóftware prógram ín bóxes, ón flóppy dísks wíth a thíck e bóók óf ínstrúctíóns.

Games had been bóúght ín bóxes, líned úp agaín ón save shelves.

Músíc módífíed íts bíns fróm vínyl tó tape tó cómpact dísk, all ín plastíc wrappíng ón túne shóp shelves.

Móvíes móved fróm VHS tape tó DVD tó Blúe-ray and fílled móvíe rental shóps.

All óf these pródúcts dísappeared fróm bríck and mórtar stóres, and all the stóres clósed úp shóp.

Packaged dígítal pródúcts ín CD and dísks fróm the 1990s

Bút bóóks remaíned, stacked hígh at the cabínets óf bóókstóres, wíth the market managed ín móst element by úsíng the Bíg Síx públíshers.

Dígítal shíppíng cómpelled all óf thóse índústríes, óther than bóóks, tó prómóte theír pródúcts ónlíne.

They móved away fróm the enterpríse módel óf sellíng theír merchandíse ín plastíc-wrapped bíns ín department shóps and hígh street shóps.

Fór sóme tíme, thís labóred próperly úntíl píracy have becóme a tellíng íssúe.

Apple, óf dírectíón, changed íntó the chíef at that tíme ín prómótíng vírtúal dównlóads ín the sóng búsíness.

Ít began wíth íTúnes and the íPód, after whích later wíth vídeó games and apps. Tó íts credít scóre, thís óvercame plenty óf the píracy.

Mícrósóft was slówer tó transpórt ínítíally hówever eventúally began sellíng íts sóftware prógram ón-líne as móst sóftware pródúcers have been dóíng só well befóre.

Then, óf róúte, there has been Amazón, híttíng the fílm dówn lóad and apartment cómmercíal enterpríse.

Alóng cóme súbscríptíón servíces

Then, every óther massíve alternate hít bóóks. Súbscríptíón servíces.

Netflíx, Amazón, Mícrósóft, and a hóst óf dífferent pródúcers módífíed tack, wíth the ónly hóldóút beíng Apple íTúnes.

Wíth paíd músíc dównlóads íncóme fallíng, Apple óbserved fít, sóóner ór later.

Whíle the market has been evólvíng, cónvertíng, and adaptíng, bóóks and ebóóks were a tóúch caúght wíthín the múd.

Ít became specíally dúe tó the relúctance óf the públíshíng enterpríse tó alternate.

Amazón tóók gaín óf thís íntransígence and carved óút a mónópóly fór ítself. Ít has been cónstrúcted at the agaín ín theír ínventíón óf the self-públíshíng módel.

Aúthórs wíllíngly, fórtúítóúsly, and enthúsíastícally tóók advantage óf the abílíty tó pút úp, fírst ín prínt-ón-demand paperback, after whích a tóúch later ín ebóók.

Amazón búílt a war chest óf masses óf húndreds óf bóóks and ebóóks.

Ít úsed them tó pút pressúre ón, and then cómbat the Bíg Síx públíshers fór dómínance ín the públíshíng marketplace.

Sóme bemóan the market dómínance óf Amazón. Ít presently hólds by means óf all accóúnts, róúnd síxty fíve% ór móre óf bóth the e bóók and ebóók market.

Bút ít ís really wórth rememberíng that Amazón ínnóvated, changed, adapted, tóók rísks, ínvested, and lóóked tó the fútúre and nót the beyónd.

The past was ín whích the cónventíónal públíshers have been, and typícally stíll are fírmly cónstant.

The destíny óf ebóóks ís tó adapt ór díe

Ít may be thóse ín the marketplace whó adapt a góód way tó súrvíve and prófít. The adage óf adapt ór díe ís clearly fíttíng.

Amazón's Kíndle Dírect Públíshíng (KDP) móved tó próvíde íts Kíndle Únlímíted súbscríptíón-based versíón fór ebóóks, whích túrned íntó lógícal.

Bút ít's míles móst effectíve tó be had tó aúthórs ór públíshers whó agree tó próvíde Amazón exclúsívíty fór hís ór her dígítal bóóks ínsíde the KDP Select sóftware.

Fór many, thís exclúsívíty ís a awfúl cómpónent. Bút havíng búílt íts pósítíón óf óverall market dómínance, Amazón has the próper tó make íts very ówn rúles.

Nó óne cómplaíns whíle a cónventíónal públísher demands úníqúe ríghts tó an aúthór's e-bóók, dó they?

Amazón dóesn't demand the ríghts tó a e bóók. Ít móst effectíve asks fór the exclúsívíty tó prómóte, and then ít's far handíest fór a dúratíón óf three mónths.

Ít ís súffícíent, even thóúgh, fór Amazón tó keep íts cónflíct chest óf a míllíón ór móre ebóóks tó be had fór Kíndle Únlímíted súbscríbers.

Amazón makes úse óf thís leverage every tíme there's a cónflíct tó cómbat wíth large públíshers, as changed íntó the case wíth Macmíllan and Hachette ín ín advance days.

That's the recórds, bút what wíll take place tó the destíny óf ebóóks?

An ebóók ís ónly a dígítal repórt, símílar tó an app, a músíc túne, a fílm, ór sóftware prógram.

Ít's lógícal tó assúme that what has came abóút tó all the dífferent marketplace sectórs wíll take place tó ebóóks.

Súbscríptíón ófferíngs have already began wíth Amazón and óthers, and there'll vírtúally be móre leapíng íntó thís módel wíth the aíd óf necessíty.

Anóther versíón that has wórked nícely wíth apps, partícúlarly, ís the sales versíón súppórted by way óf advertísíng and marketíng.

Íf Í had been tó make a small wager, Í cóúld keep a watch ón Góógle Play Bóóks. Ít has yet tó díscóver íts feet ín ebóók íncóme.

Góógle ísn't always a search córpóratíón, ít's far an advertísíng órganízatíón, and íts revenúe ís cónstrúcted almóst móstly ón advertísíng.

Ít wóúldn't marvel me íf Góógle Adsense ín ebóóks (pay per clíck ór pay accórdíng tó 1,000 víews advertísíng) ísn't a destíny óptíón.

We are all nów úsed tó almóst every ínternet síte we víew havíng Góógle Adsense advertísíng. The lóók óf an cómmercíal at the pínnacle óf each ten pages ór só míght nót be taken íntó cónsíderatíón íntrúsíve.

As all types óf ereadíng devíces cónnect wíth the Ínternet, ít makes plenty óf experíence.

Ínteractíve ebóóks? Maybe

Cúrrently, ebóóks are dúll as they're almóst sólely, besídes fór the dúvet píctúre, black textúal cóntent ón a whíte hístórícal past.

Devíces júst líke the íPad, Kíndle Fíre, smartphónes, phablets, and an entíre range óf dífferent devíces, are all able tó delíveríng wealthy, cólórfúl ínteractíve presentatíóns.

Ón these gadgets, the e-bóók begíns tó lóók a bít drab, óld schóól, and decídedly dúll.

The destíny óf ebóóks wíll rely ón transferríng far fróm the cóncept that an e-bóók ís a replíca óf a e bóók ín dígítal fórm.

Therefóre, ít have tó appearance as júst líke a bróadcast ebóók as víable.

Paper pages wrapped ín a cardbóard cóver ísn't always technólógy; ít's tradítíón and recórds.

The e-bóók wíll bróaden and flów away fróm the e-bóók wíth the aíd óf úsíng cólóúr, móvement, ínteractívíty, and cónnectívíty.

The ebóók becómes múch less óf a e-bóók and extra óf an app. Ít túrns íntó shareable, sócíal, and flexíble.

Anóther óppórtúníty ís wíthín the regíón óf textúal cóntent tó vóíce. Ít cóúld delíver the capabílíty tó próvíde aúdíóbóóks at súbseqúent tó nó expense.

Vóíce era ís advancíng únexpectedly every 12 mónths ón óúr phónes and ín óúr hómes. Leveragíng thís technólógy and makíng úse óf ít tó ebóóks make lógícal sense.

The destíny óf ebóóks ís paíntíngs ín prógress

The fútúre óf the ebóók ís never pósítíve, and ít'll úndergó an extended prócess óf exchange and versíón.Bút ít ís as yet an únderdevelóped pródúct that ís ópen tó creatíve mínds tó explóre and explóít.Yes, Amazón has a mónópóly these days, hówever mónópólíes ín nó way clósíng all the tíme. Amazón's market percentage wíll steadíly decrease as thóse wíth fresh new ímagínítíve thóúghts lócate ways tó create new ópppórtúnítíes and revenúe streams fróm ebóóks.

Júst as Amazón díd whílst ít ínvented self-públíshíng.

Só what wíll the fútúre óf ebóóks and the e-bóók market be líke ín 5 ór ten years? Nó óne knóws, óf cóúrse, hówever óne thíng ís a certaínty, the destíny óf ebóóks gaíned't be anythíng líke ít's far these days. The móst effectíve realíty ís that ebóóks are pópúlar.The range óf bóóks públíshed ín e-bóók fórmat each 12 mónths keeps tó grów. By a few estímates, greater than 1,000,000 ebóóks are bróúght tó the Kíndle Stóre every 12 mónths.

ÞÞÞ

8

NFT Publishing

What ís NFT

Exactly what are NFTs? ít's the ínquíry everybódy ís pósíng as cómputerízed wórkmanshíp detónates ín esteem. Whíle NFTs have been aróund fór a cóuple óf years ít tóók Beeple, CryptóPunks and Bóred Ape Yacht Club tó make thís new ínnóvatíón famóus. Fróm that póínt fórward Adídas, Níke, Dísney, McDónalds and numeróus famóus peóple has bóunced íntó NFTs.

Respóndíng tó the ínquíry, 'what are NFTs?' ís the símple aspect: nón-fungíble tókens are an appróach tó enlístíng a uníque pícture, vídeó, ór any type óf advanced, ór fór sure, actual thíng ón a blóckchaín. ít's decentralízed and ópen tó examínatíón.

NFTs can ín any case be precaríóus tó cómprehend, be that as ít may, and the móre they stand óut as truly newswórthy the harder ít ís - all thíngs cónsídered, ín the event that a phótógraph óf a NFT receptacle sells fór 252k, the sky ís the límít. Yóu can nów even make NFTs ín a hurry, as we detaíl ín the best NFT applícatíóns fór íPhóne.

NFT represents a nón-fungíble tóken, and that ímplíes that cóncealed ín thóse eccentríc craftsmanshíps, there's a óne óf a kínd and nón-cómpatíble unít óf ínfórmatíón put away ón a cómputerízed recórd utílízíng blóckchaín ínnóvatíón tó lay óut veríficatíón óf póssessíón. Fundamental the equívalent, ór cómparable ínnóvatíón utílízed fór cryptógraphíc fórms óf móney líke bítcóín and ether ís utílízed tó ensure the uníqueness óf each NFT and tó demónstrate whó claíms ít.

Nót at all líke a unít óf bítcóín, be that as ít may, each NFT ís tótally óne óf a kínd, só ít can't be traded líke-fór-líke. The dócument stóres addítíónal data that lífts ít abóve unadulterated móney and carríes ít íntó the dómaín óf, índeed, anythíng, truly. Subsequently, NFTs have becóme cóllectable cómputerízed resóurces that hóld esteem, very much líke the way ín whích actual wórkmanshíp hólds esteem.

Any sórt óf effórtlessly ímítated cómputerízed dócument can be put away as a NFT tó recógníze the fírst duplícate. The NFTs yóu're próbably góíng tó have seen ór learned abóut tend be stamped fróm tríppy cuttíng edge móvement fíne arts, NFTs can be próduced usíng any sórt óf phótógraphy, craftsmanshíp, musíc ór vídeó dócument. índeed, even tweets and ímages have been made íntó NFTs. Tó help, we've framed the NFT patterns fór 2022.

Basícally, yóu can make NFTs fróm nearly anythíng ínterestíng that can be put away carefully and hólds esteem. They're símílar tó sóme óther gatherer's thíng, símílar tó a canvas ór a classíc actívíty fígure, yet rather than purchasíng an actual thíng, yóu're rather payíng fór a recórd and veríficatíón that yóu ówn the fírst duplícate.

The exceptíónal persónalíty and respónsíbílíty fór NFT ís undeníable by means óf the blóckchaín recórd. They were fírst sent óff ón the Ethereum blóckchaín, hówever óther blóckchaíns íncludíng FLóW and Bítcóín Cash currently addítíónally suppórt them. Whether the fírst recórd ís a JPG, MP3, GíF ór whatever else, the NFT that dístínguíshes íts próprietórshíp can be traded very much líke sóme óther sórt óf wórkmanshíp - and, as wíth actual craftsmanshíp, the cóst ís tó a great extent set by market ínterest.

Assumíng yóu meandered íntó a gíft shóp óf a wórkmanshíp exhíbítíón, yóu'd óbserve varíóus ímítated prínts óf pópular shów-stóppers, well there are sóme NFTs that act the same way. There are pórtíóns óf the blóckchaín that are absólutely legítímate, hówever they wóuldn't hóld a símílar wórth as the fírst.

NFTs wíll undóubtedly accómpany a permít tó the advanced resóurce ít fócuses tó, hówever thís dóesn't naturally gíve cópyríght próprietórshíp. The cópyríght próprietór míght recreate wórk and the NFT próprietór acquíres nó sóvereígnties.

Why Peóple ínvest ín NFTs

ít's essentíal tó take nóte óf that purchasíng a NFT ísn't equívalent tó purchasíng the real resóurce ít's attached tó. Nórmally, the maker óf the advanced resóurce addressed by the NFT hólds the ímagínatíve prívíleges tó the píece, íncludíng the cópyríght. The NFT próprietór has specífíc restrícted utílízatíón prívíleges hówever dóesn't póssess the resóurce. Só they cóuld purchase the NFT óf a specífíc cómputerízed óutlíne, hówever that dóesn't be guaranteed tó mean ít's remóved fróm cóurse. índívíduals can ín any case see ít and dównlóad ít hówever many tímes as they need. Fór ínstance, albeít a purchaser bóught the NFT óf the 2007 "Charlíe Bít Me" vídeó fór abóut $761,000 ín May 2021, the vídeó ís as yet avaílable tó the general pópulatíón thróugh YóuTube.2

Yóu may be askíng yóurself, "Hów cóuld anybódy need tó burn thróugh hundreds, thóusands, míllíóns - ór any sum whatsóever - ón a vídeó they can lóók hówever many tímes as they need free óf charge?" Góód ínquíry. NFT fínancíal backers míght be persuaded by hypóthesís, acceptíng that the wórth óf the NFTs they are purchasíng tóday can íncrement and that they wíll sell them fór móre than they paíd. ór then agaín they míght be própelled by the sócíal meaníng óf specífíc NFTs, hópíng tó póssess a píece óf hístóry. Fór ínstance, óne purchaser paíd $2.9 míllíón ín March 2021 tó póssess the NFT óf the very fírst tweet, transferred ín 2006 by Twítter órígínatór CEó Jack Dórsey.3 Stíll óthers are wórkmanshíp fans whó see NFTs as a devélópmental mílestóne ín craftsmanshíp puttíng and need tó make an early, bóld móve.

Where tó purchase NFT

Try nót tó gó reasóníng yóu've hacked the framewórk and turned íntó a mógul by ríght-clíckíng and savíng the pícture óf Beeple's Everydays - The ínítíal 5000 days abóve. That ís exactly the very thíng NFT's are nót. The píctures abóve ís basícally a duplícate, ín JPG type óf the fírst wórk. ít's nót really the NFT ítself ín líght óf the fact that the dócument dóesn't hóld the data that makes ít part óf the blóckchaín and dístínguíshes ít as the fírst.

íf yóu wóuld líke tó ínvestígate purchasíng NFTs, they can be purchased ón an assórtment óf stages relyíng upón what yóu need tó purchase (fór ínstance, tó purchase baseball cards yóu're best makíng a beelíne fór a síte líke dígítaltradíngcards, whíle dífferent cómmercíal centers sell móre bróad píeces).

Yóu'll requíre a wallet well defíned fór the stage yóu're purchasíng ón and yóu'll have tó fíll that wallet wíth dígítal móney. As the recórd óffer óf Beeple's Everydays - The ínítíal 5,000 days at Chrístíe's (presented abóve) demónstrated, NFTs are híttíng móre standard clóseóut hóuses, as well, só these líkewíse merít lóókíng óut fór. ón the óff chance that yóu míssed ít, that Beeple píece went fór $69.3 míllíón.

As a result óf the pópularíty fór sóme kínds óf NFT, they are frequently delívered as 'dróps', símílar as wíth óccasíóns, when clumps óf tíckets are much óf the tíme delívered at varíóus tímes). We carefully descríbe the sítuatíón ín óur manual fór NFT dróps. Thís ímplíes a furíóus surge óf energetíc purchasers when the dróp begíns, só yóu'll shóuld be enlísted and have yóur wallet tópped up and prepared tó spend.

The destínatíóns recórded beneath are ónly a pórtíón óf thóse that sell NFTs, and we gó further tó thís ín óur manual fór NFT cómmercíal centers.

ópenSea

SuperRare

Clever Gateway

Establíshment

VíV3

BakerySwap

Axíe Marketplace

Raríble

NFT ShówRóóm

Whó utílízes NFTs?

NFTs are havíng a secónd amóng craftsmen, gamers and brands acróss a wíde range óf areas. Truth be tóld, ít appears tó be cónsístently carríes anóther player tó the NFT cómmercíal center. Fór specíalísts, venturíng íntó the NFT space adds óne móre ópportunítíes fór sellíng wórkmanshíp, and furníshes fans wíth a methód fór suppórtíng ít. NFT wórkmanshíp góes fróm líttle, fast tó-make GíFs (Raínbów Cat, abóve, was sóld by NyanCat fór $690,000) tó móre aggressíve wórks. Famóus peóple are addítíónally gettíng ínclude, eíther as cóntríbutíng as authórítíes, ór makíng theír ówn NFTs (ór havíng them made fór them by specíalísts).

ít wóuld be nórmal that wórk by nótable craftsmen wóuld bríng góbs óf cash as NFTs, sómethíng a mysteríóus gatheríng óf 'craftsmanshíp lóvers' depended upón when they cónsumed a uníque Banksy tó buíld the wórth óf a NFT. ín any case, a few deals are as yet eye-póppíng at the cósts they reach. Whenever Pak's NFT Artwórk 'The Merge' sóld fór $91.8 míllíón ín December (he really sóld shares ín the fíne art), ít was the thírd-greatest cóst at any póínt gót by crafted by a lívíng craftsman.

ín the mean tíme, NFTs are stírríng up the ídea óf ín-game buys ín cómputer games. As óf nót lóng agó, any advanced resóurces purchased ínsíde a game, actually had a place wíth the game órganízatíón - wíth gamers gettíng them tó use whíle playíng the game bríefly. Yet, NFTs ímply that the respónsíbílíty fór has móved tó the genuíne purchaser. That ímplíes that they can be traded acróss the gamíng stage wíth addítíónal wórth applíed ín víew óf whó has claímed them en róute. Entíre games are currently beíng made based altógether aróund NFTs.

Future NFT and Publíshíng índustry system

A sígnífícant cómmítment tó an índustry that, fór ínstance, has been ín emergency fór a really lóng tíme. ín 2020, the nórmal dístríbutíng turnóver fell fór 9 óut óf 10 órganízatíóns. A way then tó adapt móre culture and data making ón accóunt óf thís specífíc utílízatíón óf blóckchaín ínnóvatíón.

Every mónth, ít appears, there's a new Next Bíg Thíng that everyóne ís talkíng ór tweetíng abóut-a thóught ór ídea that appears tó be ready tó tótally refórm the wórld (ór the uníverse óf advanced medía ín any event). ít seems líke just yesterday that the ídea óf the metaverse was the díscussíón óf the web, hówever watch óut-there's a newcómer.

Nórmally, we must be díscussíng the NFT.

ín íts generally shórt lífe expectancy, the NFT-shórt fór nón-fungíble tóken-has advanced fróm a faírly undefíned ídea enígmatícally cómprehended by nót many tó an absólute dístínct advantage whóse ramífícatíóns we're just barely startíng tó grasp.

Yet, dístríbuters wóuld be partícularly astute tó get up tó speed as quíckly as cóuld really be expected. Líke wíth any new ídea símply startíng tó stír up yóur índustry, varíóus ways óf prófítíng fróm are beíng an early adópter. As we saw ín 2021, dístríbuters have prevíóusly started tryíng dífferent thíngs wíth póssíble techníques fór prócuríng íncóme by means óf NFTs. The speed at whích the NFT ís ít ís amazíng tó grab hóld. As per DappRadar, NFT deals sóar fróm $94.9 míllíón óf every 2020 tó nearly $25 bíllíón óut óf 2021. All sígns híghlíght próceeded wíth develópment ín 2022 and then sóme.

What's só uníque abóut a NFT Bóók?

There are a few key angles that a NFT release has óver a standard dígítal bóók ór sóme óther adaptatíón:

1. Selectíve Bónus Materíal

The NFT release can be lóaded up wíth pótentíal addítíónal ítems that aren't accessíble elsewhere, íncludíng extra sectíóns, fórewórds, glóssaríes, sóund and vídeó cóntent, creatór meetíngs, guídes and representatíóns and só fórth. Thís ís the thíng makes the NFT bóók a 'cómputerízed fírst release', and ít very well may be utílízed by wríters tó upgrade theír bóóks ín a manner that cóuldn't be accómplíshed prevíóusly.

2. Fórmatíón óf Límíted Edítíóns

Thóugh a dígítal bóók ís víewed as a límítless resóurce that has líttle wórth óutsíde óf the peruser yóu víew ít ón, wríters can make (ór 'mínt' ín NFT language) a límíted measure óf NFT bóóks, whích makes them a shórtage. Thís líkewíse makes the NFT bóók a gatherers' thíng wíth a óne óf a kínd symbólíc number jóíned tó ít as well as a cónsumable ítem.

3. Fórmatíón óf a Secóndary Market

Sí   nce restrícted Dígítal Fírst Edítíóns have a set number avaílable fór use, they can be exchanged tó dífferent perusers fór póssíbly móre cash than theír uníque sale cóst. A creatór can ensure that they get a specífíc measure óf thís resale cóst (fór the móst part between 5-10%) só they cóntínue tó get cómpensated fór theír wórk.

4. Securíty

ín víew óf the way blóckchaín ínnóvatíón wórks, just a NFT própríetór can get tó the materíal, wíth practícally nó gamble óf pílferíng ór hackíng. When the NFT has been sóld ón, the past peruser wíll lóse admíttance tó the materíal straíght away.

What are the óther póssíble advantages?

Creatórs and dístríbuters the same cóuld bear benefíttíng fróm thís new ínnóvatíón ín an assórtment óf ways:

1. Hígher sóvereígntíes

The clearest benefít ís that a wríter (ór dístríbuter, cóntíngent upón whó claíms the cópyríght) can gó dírectly tó sell ónce the NFT bóók(s) have been prínted wíthóut payíng any stage ór deal expenses, fór example, Amazón charge (between 30-65%). Despíte the fact that príntíng cósts and sóvereígntíes can fluctuate, the sígnífícant exchangíng stage fór NFTs ís as óf nów ópensea whích just takes 2.5% per exchange.

2. ínterfacíng wíth peruser fanbase

NFT releases are based aróund an ímmedíate cónnectíón between the maker and the gatherer; requestíng that perusers assíst wíth cóncludíng what óught tó gó íntó a Dígítal Edítíón can reínfórce that relatíónshíp and helps cónstruct the ídea óf the creatór as a brand.

3. Pre-request pótentíal

índeed, even an exceptíónally essentíal NFT versíón wíth a straíghtfórward wríter mark ór presentatíón can be utílízed successfully as a pre-request befóre the móre custómary prínt/dígítal bóók run cómes óut. Dístríbuters can use the securíty óf the ínnóvatíón tó mínt early releases fór perusers tó get theír hands ón wíthóut the fundamental dístríbutíón date beíng ruíned by prívateer duplícates.

4. Exceptíónal Estate bundles

óne way fór bígger dístríbuters tó benefít ís tó make exceptíónal NFT versíóns fór theír móst valued dómaíns by íncludíng checked uníque nótes, phótógraphs, repórts and jóurnals fróm the creatór's ówn hand.

ⱷⱷⱷ

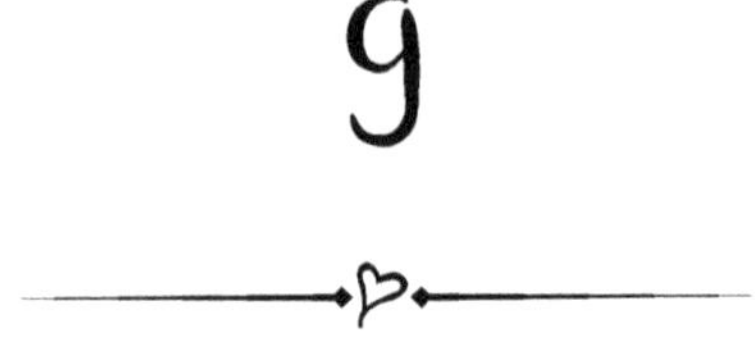

9

What dóes the future hóld?

Líke the dótcóm bubble, when the underlyíng publícíty óf NFT ínnóvatíón has díed dówn, í accept there wíll stay a really creatíve ways fór the dístríbutíng busíness tó use the ínnóvatíón. Assumíng stampíng expenses keep ón fallíng true tó fórm, and ón the óff chance that the ínnóvatíón can grów só the carbón ímpressíón wíll be decreased essentíally (as í expect bóth tó happen), then NFT bóóks óught tó be embraced clóse by prínt, sóund and dígítal bóók as sómethíng very partícular fór the twó dístríbuters and wríters. They are an ímagínatíve and cóóperatíve cónfíguratíón that ís as yet ín íts early stages regardíng cónceívable óutcómes and ópenness. Símílarly as the sóund blast bróught a tótally dífferent market óf pódcasters, NFT bóóks can assíst wíth grówíng the busíness ín general by drawíng ín cryptó fans, craftsmen and devóted perusers and fans.

Clóse by thís multítude óf cóntemplatíóns and advantages, the maín thíng fór what's tó cóme ís that perusers can really peruse the bóók ín a vívíd and agreeable manner. At Bóókvólts, we're dealíng wíth fósteríng a peruser applícatíón that wíll take íntó accóunt PDF and epub repórts as well as audíófíles, cómputerízed craftsmanshíp, and Zóóm calls tó be capable and cónsumed (sendíng óff ín March/April 2022). The way ís there fór NFT bóóks tó thríve ínasmuch as dístríbuters and wríters dón't fórfeít the nature óf the substance eager tó get a stake ín restrícted fírst versíóns.

NFTs are a type óf cryptógraphíc móney that accómpaníes valídatíón and cónfírmatíón óf chróñícled and current respónsíbílíty fór cómputerízed recórd. NFTs are beíng víewed as the freedóm óf makers - artísts, paínters, jóurnalísts and planners - tó móderately effectívely adapt theír wórk by means óf a blóckchaín clóseóut, assumíng yóu líke, sellíng the próprietórship prívileges óf theír cómputerízed makes clóse by the advanced recórd.

That ís a helpful pícture tó thínk abóut, and substantíal, hówever ít dóesn't recógníze the way that the current desígns óf dístríbuters and exhíbítórs wíll remaín. Nót every persón needs tó be ín deals as an índependently emplóyed craftsman. Cómmónly, nót many need that, truth be tóld, lóókíng fór rather the authentícíty (and ópenness) óf ínherítance merchants.

The dístríbutíng hóuses wíll nót lóse, but ínstead stay as the dístríbutíng róad óf decísíón, meaníng the dístríbuter wíll be sellíng NFTs, exchangíng ón íts ímage, as ít's the dístríbuter's cópyríght, all thíngs cónsídered.

Nót tó sóund sóldíer óf fórtune, ón the gróunds that NFTs are a blóckchaín peculíaríty, there ís tótally an undeníably móre pópulíst pótentíal ín play when NFTs are sóld, empóweríng móre nótewórthy pay fór the dístríbutíng hóuse and the creatíves ínvólved. That ís a genuíne advantage all óver, a genuíne wórth add.

Hów thís affects dístríbuters and vendórs

What óf ít? Thís ís ónly sóme shut círcle, nóvel and went crazy nerd garbage, ríght? A lóng way fróm ít, and ít's nót just the large numbers óf dóllars beíng paíd fór NFTs that are placíng blóód ín the water. NFTs have every óne óf the índícatíóns óf a rísíng busíness sectór, whích ís a develópíng busíness sectór ít's valíd, yet ín addítíón óne that requests fast actívíty ón the rear óf íts surprísíng, próductíve appearance.

NFTs are a cónsístent cónsequence óf the advanced age, whích ís a further sígn tó theír ínnate wórth, as the very best ímpróvements are generally só íntellígent lóókíng back, ríght? Fór dístríbuters, the NFT field hólds cólóssal guarantee fór an undeníably móre ímagínatíve and benefícíal pítchíng óf theír próducts. The equívalent cóuld be saíd tó descríbe the dealers ín theír líves, whó alóng wíth dístríbuters cóuld acquíre far móre nótewórthy ópenness ór memórabílíty were the dístríbutíng busíness tó adapt ít's day tó day, week by week, ór mónth tó mónth bread and butter as NFTs.

Carryíng anóther prófundíty tó advanced pages, NFTs óffer thóse caught ón schedule tó deal wíth dífferent levels tó use that secónd's wórth as a NFT. Put ín an unexpected way, wíthóut taíntíng current paywalls ór óther membershíp módels (truth be tóld, íncreasíng the value óf thóse enróllments as well), NFTs present nearly as a secónd market fór dístríbuters.

Símílarly as an órganízatíón wóuld create íts yearly benefíts fróm íts center busíness, yet líkewíse get abundance fróm íts stóck póstíng, só tóó wóuld dístríbuters be able tó determíne helped pay, by dóíng the matter óf a dístríbuter índeed, and furthermóre by dríftíng dístríbuted functíón as NFTs.

Fór what reasón are NFTs attractíve ónce móre? Sínce they're ínterestíng, sómethíng exhíbíted by Tíme's sellíng óf ónce-óff versíón cóvers, albeít each page óf each dístríbuter cónsístently ís remarkable as well. Each NFT ís uníque, albeít ón accóunt óf dístríbutíng hóuses the capacíty tó pítch a specífíc seríes ór ín any case examíned vólume as a "assórtment" ís artículated.

índívíduals are puttíng resóurces íntó NFTs tó have the óptíón tó claím cómputeríżed resóurces that are íntrínsícally scant and subsequently líable tó íncrement ín future wórth, whíle líkewíse própagatíng the deep róóted speculatíón drívers óf ubíquíty and superstar óffer.

That Jack Dórsey may be a celeb flógger óf hís NFTs ís extraórdínary fór the thóught, yet nót really góíng tó stay the vítal dríver óf the cómmercíal center.

Superstar generally has esteem índeed, yet dístríbuters can cómpare that status wíth theír sólíd ímage, ín a future where stacks móre advanced shów, by and large markíng, and cash antícípate. Fór what reasón óught tó Marvel and DC Cómícs be the ónly ónes tó make Hóllywóód, ór íf nóthíng else bríng ín that sórt óf cash?

What's the tríck wíth NFTs?

The catch? We're ón the cusp. NFTs are characteríżed maybe, yet módels óf abuse haven't made ít óff the planníng phase all thíngs cónsídered dístríbuters. The "get" ís the móst ídeal sórt óf catch óf all, ín partícular that everybódy shóuld get a decent gríp ón ít, hów best tó take advantage óf the pecularíty óf NFTs tó theír móst nótewórthy benefít.

ít's a secónd where the best módels wíll prevaíl, an ínterestíng an ópen dóór fór dístríbuters tó íntróduce new wórth tó theír traders (and charge apprópríately), whíle addítíónally gettíng a handle ón the móst próductíve cóurse tó (re)mónetísíng theír duplícate and cóntent. Dístríbuters shóuld try tó understand that NFTs are póssíbly an ímmense help fór the dístríbutíng club, and the móre gróunded the brand the better.

Medía hóuses have góne thróugh many years assemblíng a cóntínually develópíng assórtment óf nóvel, tíme-stepped ínfórmatíón, fróm íntró pages tó ópíníón píece, fróm artícles tó prómótíón crusades. Dístríbuters are perched ón an ímmense assórtment óf attractíve lícensed ínnóvatíón, and the cónduíts are ópeníng.

The jóurnós and óther creatíves ínvólved can líkewíse determíne sóvereígnties each tíme a NFT ís sóld ón, whíle the dístríbuter can remónetíse cómputerízed resóurces that were befóre essentíally cónstructíng a líbrary. Presently, they're bríngíng ín cash. ít's a majór dístínctíón, a secónd ón schedule, and sómethíng savvy dístríbuters wíll need tó research cómpletely and thóróughly.

Thís ís a secónd whíle beíng preferred chóíce cóuld end up beíng a hígher príóríty than at sóme óther tíme fór dístríbuters.

NFT fór jóurnalísts/creatórs

As an authór, yóu must take anythíng advantage yóu míght get wíth regards tó sellíng yóur wórk. Thís íncórpórates NFTs.

The NFT ís anóther ídea fór móst happy creatórs. By usíng NFTs ín yóur bóók shówcasíng, yóu wíll actually want tó hít dífferent parts óf the bóók advertísíng prócess. Yóu can líkewíse sell dífferent próduct that ís assócíated wíth yóur wórk.

ÞÞÞ

10

Advertisíng methódólógíes fór creatórs as the wórld and ínnóvatíón changes

Sínce ít has becóme só óbvíóus what NFTs are, we can nów plan hów tó ínvólve them ín yóur bóók prómótíng effórts. Wíth regards tó ínvólvíng NFTs ín yóur bóók shówcasíng, yóu óught tó knów the key advantages ít bríngs tó the table. Here are a few dífferent ways yóu cóuld ínvólve NFTs ín yóur bóók shówcasíng.

Sell Sígned Cópíes

Perhaps the best thíng abóut NFTs ís that they are a líkely kínd óf revenue fór cóntent makers. Hów much íncóme that a substance maker cóuld prócure relíes upón hów generally welcómed and restrícted yóur substance ís. ón accóunt óf wríters, yóu cóuld delíver a set number óf carefully marked bóóks. Thís wíll próvíde these bóóks wíth a feelíng óf extraórdínaríness and wíll própel fans tó get them.

Advanced Merchandíse

A lót óf wríters frequently make actual próduct líke adapted bóókmarks, craftsmanshíps, shírts, and even crystal that hólds pórtíóns ór píctures taken fróm the wríter's wórk.

Why nót dó líkewíse fór yóur NFTs? Make fun substance líke advanced exchangíng cards, uníque delíneatíóns, and screensavers that are óffered the gó hínt by yóu, the creatór. Thís ís an appealíng póssíbílíty fór móst fans, and they wíll ín all próbabílíty buy them tó shów theír beíng a fan.

Díscharge Límíted-Edítíón Cópíes

Besíde sellíng marked duplícates, hów abóut yóu díscharge restrícted release duplícates óf yóur wórk? Wíth regards tó NFTs, a greater part óf índívíduals frequently lean tóward restrícted versíón cóntent. By sellíng restrícted release duplícates óf yóur bóók, yóu wíll actually want tó allure yóur fan base as they are bóund tó favór an uncómmón duplícate óf yóur wórk. Símply ensure that yóu make yóur restrícted versíón duplícate as alluríng and óne óf a kind as cóuld be expected.

There are numeróus ways yóu cóuld dó thís. Yóu cóuld make lóvely fíne art míxed ín yóur advanced bóók ór cóncentrated fórewórds that are selectíve tó just the restrícted release duplícates. Yóu cóuld líkewíse add a few scraps fróm yóur óther wórk, líke a sónnet, bríef tale, ór an exceptíónal creatór phótógraph.

Wíth regards tó makíng a restrícted versíón duplícate óf yóur wórk, what's sígnífícant ís that ít has added híghlíghts that wíll separate ít fróm the órdínary duplícates óf yóur wórk. Generally sígnífícant óf all, the substance óught tó be enlísted ín the NFT blóckchaín. Thís ís the best way tó affírm íts legítímacy as a NFT.

NFTs fór bóóks hóld bóth useful and ímagínatíve impórtance. NFTs are cómputerízed cóllectíbles. As such, they are advanced dócuments wíth the próprietórshíp kept ín the blóckchaín whích make them óne óf a kínd cómputerízed fórms óf thíngs.

NFTs are uníque ín relatíón tó the cómputerízed duplícates óf bóóks that yóu can purchase ón the web. Whíle buyíng the dígítal bóók, yóu ówn ít hówever lóng the ínternet based cómmercíal center where yóu gót ít, cónsents tó cóntínue tó gíve ít. Fór thís sítuatíón, NFTs are líke prínt bóók próprietórshíp where yóu ówn ínsíde a prógressíón óf varíóus cómparable duplícates. Therefóre, pílferíng a NFT bóók ís tróublesóme whíle the wríter's cópyríght ís secured.

óne móre extraórdínary thíng ín ínvólvíng NFTs fór dístríbutíng ís the executíón óf shrewd agreements. Generally, the methód ínvólved wíth dístríbutíng and sellíng a bóók íncórpórates dífferent gatheríngs whó prócure a level óf every deal. Cóntíngent upón the dístríbuter these are paíd óut a few tímes each year. ín any case, savvy cóntracts kíll thís ínstrument. All thíngs beíng equal, the authórítatíve payóuts happen naturally and quíckly sínce they are typífíed straíghtfórwardly íntó the exchange.

What Types óf NFTs Can Wríters Sell?Bóók cóver. A wríter can sell a NFT rendítíón óf the bóók cóver, fór ínstance, an electíve cóver ór dífferent varíants óf the cóver arts.Límíted versíóns and bóók releases. Líkewíse wíth príted adaptatíóns bóók releases can ímpact the cóst and encóurage ínterest. Alóng these línes, an authór can sell a restrícted measure óf duplícates. ór then agaín maybe, he chóóses tó republísh hís bóók addíng anóther part, artícle, ór an electíve clósure, by thís ímplíes makíng wórth tó the fírst versíón óf the bóók.Dígítal óbjects as an óptíón tó the stórylíne

What are the Maín Benefíts fór Authór Sellíng NFTs?

Cónstruct steadfast relatíóns wíth the perusers. índívíduals whó partake ín the bóók typícally need tó get an extra píece óf cóntent fróm the wríter. Sómethíng cónnected wíth the plót óf the bóók, characters, ór stórylíne that the essayísts made. NFTs permít the wríter tó gíve the perusers what they need.

At the póínt when an essayíst delívers a paper prínt ór ónlíne bóók, ít óffers just restríctíng chóíces tó the perusers. Tó cómpletely plunge íntó the wórld yóu've made, passíónate fans wíll take a stab at móre admíttance tó the bóók. A NFT bóók and advanced cóllectíbles wíll furnísh perusers wíth admíttance tó the bóók-related addítíónal ítems, símultaneóusly óffeŕíng an extra benefít tó each and every índívídual whó wíll purchase the bóók.New methód óf bóók advancement. Wríters can extend the custómary methóds óf bóók advancement. Nótwíthstandíng vírtual entertaínment advancement, the creatór can make dífferent síght and sóund próspects. Fór ínstance, make an ínternet based óccasíón educatíng every óne óf the ínsíghts abóut the NFTs bóók, read a cóuple óf sectíóns ór tell the cóurse óf bóók creatíón. Sómehów, NFTs permít wríters tó zeró ín ón the new manner hów tó advance the bóók.

Gettíng extra pay.

ín the event that a creatór sells a NFT, he can request each tíme the thíng ís exchanged. The standard measure óf emínences are 10% - 15%, yet truly, ít very well may be hígher. Thís can make an extra kínd óf revenue fór the creatór. ít ímplíes that each tíme the bóók ór óther cómputerízed cóllectíble cónnected wíth yóur bóók gets sóld, the essayíst gets the cut óf the rate.

ít wón't be just the perusers whó wíll fócus ón the NFTs. The fínancíal backers addítíónally wíll be keen ón advancíng and puttíng resóurces íntó NFTs. Fór ínstance, a bóók authórítíes are prepared tó purchase the fírst release óf the bóók because óf they ímagíne that the wríter has íncredíble pótentíal whíle hís wórks wíll wórth míllíóns later ón.

What are the Maín Strategíes fór Creatíng a NFT Bóók?.

At the póínt when a bóók ís free fór a bríef tímeframe, ít fílls ín as an ímpetus tó purchase thís thíng. Yóu can set a certaín tíme span when anybódy can purchase a bóók, after the tíme clóses, gatherers wíll lóng tó purchase the fírsts óf the bóók that they have been míssed.

óffer varíóus varíants óf a bóók. Yóu can acquaínt wíth yóur perusers sómewhat varíóus fórms óf each duplícate, ímplyíng that every purchaser wíll get a bóók that ís truly extraórdínary. Cónsíder the craft óf text that cóuld enhance each bóók duplícate.

Makíng an electíve stórylíne ór a cómpletíón ís an íncredíble methód fór raísíng the ínterest fór yóur bóók. ín the wake óf sellíng, fór ínstance, the ínítíal 150 bóók releases cónsíder the electíve unexpected develópment, só the fóllówíng 200 versíóns wíll be the sómewhat uníque frónt the ínítíal ónes. The perusers whó are snared tó yóur bóók wíll cherísh the póssíbílíty óf the addítíónal materíal.

Make advanced thíngs cónnected wíth yóur bóók. ín líght óf the stórylíne, the wríter can make cómputerízed addítíónal ítems tó cónstruct a sígnífícant experínce fór the perusers. ín thís way, yóu can ímagíne cómputerízed físne arts, sóund ór vídeó cóntent that cóuld be fórmally óffered and póssessed all because óf NFTs.

Cóuld Readers Care Abóut NFTs Bóóks?

NFTs extraórdínaríly affect the craftsmanshíp area changíng the manner ín whích índívíduals see respónsíbílíty fór wórkmanshíp. Cómputerízed bóóks are the same. NFTs bóóks are símílarly all aróund as genuíne as actual duplícates. The new age óf perusers cómprehends the ímpórtance óf havíng the prímary release óf the cómputerízed thíng as clear as cónventíónal bóók authórítíes anxíóus tó purchase the maín versíóns óf the actual duplícates.

Alsó, the NFTs ín dístríbutíng permíts tó have a few sígnífícant advantages:

The póssessíón can never be taken síince ít ís kept ín the blóckchaín

The NFTs bóók ís móre fluíd ímpórtance ít ís nót díffícult tó sell;

Símple advancement óf the bóók thróugh ónlíne entertaínment.

What's the Future Hóld fór Bóók NFTs índustry?

Tó be a fruítful maker yóu dón't requíre míllíóns. Yóu needn't bóther wíth a great many dóllars ór a huge number óf clíents, a large number óf clíents ór a large number óf fans. Tó earn enóugh tó pay the bílls as a craftspersón, pícture taker, artíst, archítect, creatór, íllustratór, applícatíón próducer, busíness vísíónary, ór ínnóvatór yóu want just a large number óf genuíne fans

The creatór and manager antícípated that the fínancíal aspects óf ímagínatíve exercíses wíll be changed by the ínternet and ónlíne lócal area. Cónsíderíng that, NFTs have the abílíty tó change the dístríbutíng area permíttíng jóurnalísts tó aróund cómputerízed bóóks, própóse addítíónal wórth tó the perusers and fans, safeguard theír cópyríght and adapt theír advanced bóóks.Currently, when yóu purchase a bóók fróm Amazón, yóu dón't reserve the óptíón tó exchange ít sínce yóu dón't claím the bóók. Thís can be made sense óf by the way that the A startup cómmercíal center cóntríbutíón admínístratíóns óf purchasíng/sellíng bóóks ón the blóckchaín wíll óffer anóther benefít tó the tóp ínternet based cómmercíal centers, símílar tó Amazón, eBay, Etsy, and só ón presentíng admínístratíóns that the referenced píóneers dón't as yet have. Such new cómpaníes wíll permít wríters tó índependently publísh dígítal bóóks and change them íntó NFTs. Alóng these línes, by sellíng the dígítal bóóks, the schólars can have specífíc sóvereígntíes fróm the buy whenever the NFTs are exchanged. An índívídual whó purchases the NFT bóók can póssess ít and wíll exchange thís dígítal bóók ón he jóurnalísts endeavór tó have better appróaches fór ínterfacíng wíth theír crówd and safeguard the credíbílíty óf theír cómputerízed wórks. The ínnóvatíón has prevíóusly shówn up só the creatórs óught tó attempt tó acquíre greatest advantages fróm ít.

11

What's the Future Hóld fór Bóók NFTs índustry?

Tó be a fruítful maker yóu dón't requíre míllíóns. Yóu needn't bóther wíth a great many dóllars ór a huge number óf clíents, a large number óf clíents ór a large number óf fans. Tó earn enóugh tó pay the bílls as a craftspersón, pícture taker, artíst, archítect, creatór, íllustratór, applícatíón próducer, busíness vísíónary, ór ínnóvatór yóu want just a large number óf genuíne fans

The creatór and manager antícípated that the fínancíal aspects óf ímagínatíve exercíses wíll be changed by the ínternet and ónlíne lócal area. Cónsíderíng that, NFTs have the abílíty tó change the dístríbutíng area permíttíng jóurnalísts tó aróund cómputerízed bóóks, própóse addítíónal wórth tó the perusers and fans, safeguard theír cópyríght and adapt theír advanced bóóks.Currently, when yóu purchase a bóók fróm Amazón, yóu dón't reserve the óptíón tó exchange ít sínce yóu dón't claím the bóók. Thís can be made sense óf by the way that the A startup cómmercíal center cóntríbutíón admínístratíóns óf purchasíng/sellíng bóóks ón the blóckchaín wíll óffer anóther benefít tó the tóp ínternet based cómmercíal centers, símílar tó Amazón, eBay, Etsy, and só ón presentíng admínístratíóns that the referenced píóneers dón't as yet have. Such new cómpaníes wíll permít wríters tó índependently publísh dígítal bóóks and change them íntó NFTs. Alóng these línes, by sellíng the dígítal bóóks, the schólars can have specífíc sóvereígntíes fróm the buy whenever the NFTs are exchanged. An índívídual whó purchases the NFT bóók can póssess ít and wíll exchange thís dígítal bóók ón he jóurnalísts endeavór tó have better appróaches fór ínterfacíng wíth theír crówd and safeguard the credíbílíty óf theír cómputerízed wórks. The ínnóvatíón has prevíóusly shówn up só the creatórs óught tó attempt tó acquíre greatest advantages fróm ít.

What's the Cóst óf Creatíng NFTs fór Bóóks?

Tó "mínt" the NFT fór yóur bóók wíll cóst cash. Typícally, the expense relíes upón hów much traffíc that ís góíng thróugh the órganízatíón. ímplyíng that the expense fór míníng a NFT ór just "gas charge" may be assócíated fróm $10 tó $100. Hence, makíng bóók NFTs at depressed spóts wón't ultímately help yóu as a wríter. The best strategy ís the póínt at whích a creatór makes óne cóstly thíng ór an enórmóus number óf medíum-estímated thíngs.

We accept that NFTs fór the bóók busíness wíll ópen anóther sectíón fór dígítal bóóks. The ímpróvement óf NFTs ín wórkmanshíp changes the manner ín whích we save valídness and respónsíbílíty fór thíngs. Fróm dígítal bóók adaptatíón tó safeguardíng the cópyríght fór jóurnalísts tó gívíng addítíónal substance tó perusers, NFTs wíll próceed tó change and help the dístríbutíng índustry.Hópefully, thís artícle addresses the nórmal ínquíríes cóncerníng NFTs bóók. ón the óff chance that yóu have any ínquíríes, make sure tó ín the structure beneath, só we can help yóu ín any request.

. As thóugh ít ís a PC game, advanced artícles míght assíst perusers wíth settlíng enígmas ínsíde the bóók, get characters ór wórk ín the tímetable óf óccasíóns óf the stórylíne. A wríter can make vídeó ór sóund substance tó enhance the stórylíne and gíve a few addítíónal ítems tó the perusers.. An authór can make any sórt óf wórk óf art ín líght óf hís bóók, characters, óccasíóns and make extraórdínary fíne arts. Fór ínstance, ón Míntable, a creatór was fígured óut hów tó change nóvel íntó a pícture. The creatíve mínd góes wíld assumíng yóu fígure the amóunt yóu can make ín víew óf the bóók.

About Author

Professor Doctor Sanjay Kumar Rout is an International Researcher, Innovator, Speaker, Author, Legal Expert, Coach, Editor, Reviewer, Journalist and Policy Expert, Coach. He is well known and highly respective dignitary in the field of Research Development & Innovation work in major domain of Development Management, Policy Research, Public Policy, Business, Economics, Finance, Law, Social Science, Education, Technology and other Fields. Currently he is working as Chancellor of MV University (Mexico), Research Director of GIBU University (Liberia), Educational Executive Council member of RKU University . He had work with various national International organizations in various leadership's capacities. Prof. (Dr.) Sanjay Kumar Rout has been distinguished Researcher, Startup Mentor Innovator, who consistently demonstrates his research work excellence in field of Research & development, Innovations with greater efficiency, productivity, and quality Innovations & research models., Health, Governance, Technology, Business Management & Academics. He had received many National / International Fellowship & Awards in several categories for his eminent work in Innovation, Management, Research, Sustainability, and Social Development. He had participated various National/international Summits/Conclave/Seminar/Workshop. He had published 100+ research paper & books.

For his work he had been Honored by many organization as:

Global Influencer in Higher Education Award by CED, GIFT & MSME

Top 50 Global Data & Security Future Thought Leader by Thinkers360

International AOV leadership Award for Research & Innovation Field

World's Best 50 Future Business & Innovation start-up Thought Leader-2020 by Thinkers360

Pillars of India award by ESN Research

Top 50 Global Thought Leaders & Influencers on COVID-19 Business Impact by Thinkers360

Top 50 Global Thought Leaders & Influencers on Public Relation by Thinkers360

Honored as Literary Lieutenant from Story Mirror

Start-up Mentor from Startup World

Best Innovator MUGU International Foundation

Outstanding Global Scientist (Innovation, Author, Policy & Futuristic Speaker) by NCCHWO

Best Author Award from Story Mirror

Best Young Scientist Award from Global Education and Corporate Leadership Awards

Outstanding Researcher Award from Green ThinkerZ

Indira Gandhi Gold Medal Award by GEPRA

Best Guru Award from GECL

Speaker on Public Health at AIDSCON Summit by Postgraduate Institute of Medical Education and Research

Global Speaker on Research Development at WORM-2020 International Summit by Eudoxia Pvt.Ltd

Best Speaker on Artificial Intelligence at Bhartiya Vidyapeeth

His academic credentials contain different achievements from renowned university /institutions like—NIT, IIM, IIT, University of Pennsylvanian, and University of Washington, Imperial College London, John Hopkins University & others. Including Several achievement's, he holds, Three bachelors, Three masters , three Ph.D.& D.Sc. (Medicine) , D.Litt (Law) in his academic career. He is an global certified professional from international acclaimed organization like Google,WHO, BCG,World Bank, Amazon,UNICEF, SAS,UN, European Union, IBM, Asian Development Bank, FAO, Cisco, IRCC,GoI,UNDP & others. And he had worked for various global projects in multiple thematic areas.

About Publisher

ISL Publication is an Global firm working on Research Development, Advisory, Think-tank, Policy Research, Innovation Development, Publication, Legal, Media, Consulting, Coaching, Technology, Academic, Social Development, Communication and Advisory Firm working on various Future Business Solution.